BATTLE OF ANGELS

BY TENNESSEE WILLIAMS

BATTLE OF ANGELS, a play in 2 acts and 3 scenes, was presented by the Theatre Guild, Inc. at the Wilbur Theatre, Boston, for two weeks, starting December 30, 1940, and ending January 11, 1941. Margaret Webster directed.

The present edition of BATTLE OF ANGELS, in 3 acts, was first presented by Circle Repertory Company at the Circle Theatre on Sheridan Square November 3, 1974. It played a scheduled limited engagement of 32 performances. It was directed by Marshall W. Mason, set design by John Lee Beatty, light design by Dennis Parichy, costumes by Jennifer von Mayrhauser, and music by Norman L. Berman.

The cast in order of appearance:

CONJURE MAN .... Lance Taylor, Jr.
DOLLY BLAND .... Sharon Madden
PEE WEE BLAND .... Baxter Harris
BEULAH CARTWRIGHT .... Rheatha Forster
SHERIFF TALBOTT .... Jack Davidson
CASSANDRA WHITESIDE .... Trish Hawkins
VEE TALBOTT .... Conchata Ferrell
VAL XAVIER .... Max (sic)
BLANCH TEMPLE .... Maryellen Flynn
EVA TEMPLE .... Berrilla Kerr
MYRA TORRANCE .... Tanya Berezin
LOON .... Elliott C. Moffitt
JABE TORRANCE .... Ron Seka
EDNA MAE .... Suzanne Golden
JANE .... Diana Malchin
SHERRI-LEE .... Julie Wakefield
DAVID ANDERSON .... Alan Jordan
BENNIE .... Matthew McDonald
TOWNSMEN .... Alan Jordan, Allan Goldstein, Alan Fox
MRS. REGAN .... Debra Mooney

TIME:
    Act One. Early February, early morning.
    Act Two. A week later, afternoon and twilight.
    Act Three. Two months later, a rainy April afternoon.

PLACE:
    Torrance Mercantile Store,
    Two River County, Mississippi.

BATTLE OF ANGELS

PROLOGUE

When the House Manager closes the doors of the store the Conjure Man plays two chords. On the third chord the house lights go out. Pee Wee enters and crosses to pinball machine. When he is on the step near it, Sheriff Talbott enters. Pee Wee shoots ball as Sheriff takes off his coat. Dolly enters on first ball, Beulah from behind when she hears door chimes. Both go to counter.

ACT ONE

SCENE: *The same as for the Prologue, except that it is now a year earlier—in early February—and the store is in operation, stocked with merchandise. There are great bolts of Pepperell and percale which stand upright on the counters. The black skeleton of a dressmaker's dummy stands meaninglessly in front of a thin white column. Along the wall at the left is the shoe department, with a ladder that slides along the shelves and two or three shoe-fitting chairs. Racks of dresses, marked "Spring Styles," line the right wall.*

Dolly and Beulah are arranging candles and setting a buffet table in the general store. They are wives of small planters, about thirty and overdressed. Dolly's husband, Pee Wee, and the town sheriff are in the confectionery shooting pinball. A train whistles in the distance.

DOLLY. Pee Wee! That's the Cannonball!

PEE WEE. *(From the confectionery.)* Okay, Mama!

*Pee Wee enters. He is a heavy man. His vest comes midway
down the white-shirted bulge of his belly; his laced boots are
caked with mud.*

Ninety-five dimes an' no pay-off! What would you call that, Mama?

DOLLY. Outrageous! Not the machine, but you poor suckers that play it.

BEULAH. This meringue turned out real good.

TALBOTT. *(Entering from the confectionery, laughing.)* You got to mid-aisle it three times straight's the only way to crack that goddam pot.

PEE WEE. I'm gonna tell Jabe about it. Ninety-five dimes an' no pay-off.

They go out.

DOLLY. I guess Jabe Torrance has got more to think about than that ole pinball game. Huh?

BEULAH. He ought to have. That meringue *is* nice and light. I put in two drops of almond. Yesterday I was talking to Dr. Bob. You know, young Dr. Bob?

DOLLY. Uh-huh. What did he say?

BEULAH. I ast him how Jabe was, what kind of condition he really seemed to be in. He's seen them X-ray pictures they took in the Memphis Hospital after the operation. Well…

DOLLY. What did he say, Beulah?

BEULAH. He said the worst that a doctor can ever say.

DOLLY. What's that?

BEULAH. Nothing at all, not a spoken word did he utter; he simply looked at me with those big dark eyes and shook his haid—like this!

DOLLY. *(Speaking with doleful optimism.)* I guess he signed Jabe Torrance's death warrant with just that single motion of his haid.

BEULAH. Exackly what I thought. I understand that they cut him open…

DOLLY. An' sewed him right back up?

BEULAH. *(Struggling to speak and strangling on an olive.)* Mmm. Mmm. *(Points at her stuffed mouth.)* I didn't know these olives had seeds in them.

DOLLY. You thought they was stuffed?

BEULAH. Uh-huh.

DOLLY. Where's the Temple Sisters?

BEULAH. Snooping around upstairs.

DOLLY. Let Myra catch 'em at it, she'll lay 'em both out good. She never did invite nobody up there.

BEULAH. Well, I was surprised when I went up myself.

DOLLY. I know it.

BEULAH. Two separate bedrooms, too! Maybe it's just since Jabe's been sick.

DOLLY. Naw, it's permanent honey. As a girl in Tupelo she certainly wasn't cold-blooded. We used to go double together, me an' Pee Wee an' her and that Anderson boy. All of one spring we would go to the orchard across from Moon Lake ev'ry night. We was engaged, but they wasn't. Myra was Myra then. Since then she's just a woman who works in a mercantile store.

> *Cassandra Whiteside enters.*

Sandra Whiteside! How are you?

SANDRA. Oh I seem to be still living. God knows why. I caught the heel of my slipper in that rotten boardwalk out there and it broke right off. They say if you break the heel of your slipper in the morning, it means you'll meet the love of your life before dark. But it was already dark when I broke the heel of my slipper. Maybe that means I'll meet the love of my life before daybreak! Where's Myra?

DOLLY. Gone to Memphis to bring Jabe back from the hospital.

BEULAH. The men folks just now went to the depot to meet them.

SANDRA. Oh. …I want some cartridges for this pistol of mine.

> *She removes it from her bag.*

I thought I better carry one with me. I'm on the road so much you'd think I was making a political campaign tour, the number of places I've got to visit this weekend. Memphis, Jackson—Is this the hardware section? (*Approaching the counter.*) Aw, here's cartridges!

> *She helps herself.*

Then on down to New Awleuns for the start of the carnival season. Tell

Myra to charge these to me. I ought to buy an airplane. They say that you only crack up once in the air.

DOLLY. Well, you'd better stay out of airplanes, honey.

BEULAH. How many times have you cracked up on the highway?

SANDRA. Today was the seventh since New Year's.

DOLLY. No!

SANDRA. I fell asleep at the wheel an' ran into a mule.

BEULAH. Goodness!

DOLLY. Gracious! My Lawd!

SANDRA. And just to show you the absolute lack of justice, the mule was killed and I was completely uninjured!

DOLLY. *(With false concern.)* Darling, you'd better be careful!

SANDRA. Oh, I don't know. What else can you do when you live in Two River County but drive like hell!

> There is the sound of a car out in front.

BEULAH. 'S 'at them?

DOLLY. *(Sarcastically.)* Naw, it's the sheriff's little fireside companion.

BEULAH. Vee Talbott! Who is that with her? A *man!*

> This word creates a visible stir among the three women.

DOLLY. Uh-huh! Yes, it is!

BEULAH. Who could it be I wonder?

DOLLY. I can't make out. Oh, my goodness! What an outfit he's got on! It looks like a snakeskin jacket.

BEULAH. *Wha-at?* Do you know him?

DOLLY. Naw, I don't know him a-tall. He looks like an absolute stranger. Poor Vee has got her skirt caught in the car door or something, it's hitched up over her knees and she's simply *frantic* about it!

> She utters a sharp laugh.

BEULAH. She's such a big clumsy thing. Who do you think the man is?

DOLLY. I told you I never have seen him, don't know him from Adam, darling. Maybe he's one of the Twelve Apostles that she's been painting on.

SANDRA. Is Vee painting the Twelve Apostles?

DOLLY. She's been painting them for twelve years, one each year. She says that she sees them in visions. But every one of them looks like some man around Two River County. She told Birdie Wilson that she was hoping she'd have a vision of Jesus next Passion Week so she could paint Him, too.

BEULAH. You better quit staring.

DOLLY. She's finally got her skirt loose. Oh, God, the hem's ripped out, it's trailing the ground!

> *She laughs and crosses from the window. Vee enters from the street. She is a heavy middle-aged woman, about forty, whose personality, frustrated in its contact with externals, has turned deeply inward. She has found refuge in religion and primitive art and has become known as an eccentric. Although a religious fanatic, a mystic, she should not be made ridiculous. Her portrayal will contain certain incidents of humor, but not be devoid of all dignity or pathos. She wanders slowly about with a vague dreamy smile on her face. Her expression is often bewildered.*

BEULAH. Hello, Vee honey, how are you?

DOLLY. Hello Vee.

VEE. I got m'skirt caught in the lock of the Chevrolet door an' I think it's torn loose a little. Is it dark in here or am I losing my eyesight? I been painting all day, finished a picture in a ten-hour stretch. Just stopped a few minutes for coffee and went back to it again while I had a clear vision. I think I got it right this time. But I'm so exhausted I could drop in my tracks. There's nothing more exhausting than that kind of work on earth. It's not so much that it tires your body out, but it leaves you drained inside. Y'know what I mean? Inside? Like you was burned out or something! Well! Still! You feel you have accomplished something when you're through with it, sometimes you feel elevated! How are you Dolly? Does it look like it's torn to you?

BEULAH. Just a little bit honey.

DOLLY. Yes, it's scarcely noticeable even.

VEE. Aw well, I'm just in time. I brought my new picture with me, the paint isn't dry on it yet. I thought Myra might want to hang it up in Jabe's room while he's convalescin' from the operation, 'cause after a close shave with death, people like to be reminded of spiritual things. Huh? Yes, this is the Holy Ghost ascending!

DOLLY. You didn't put a head on it.

VEE. The head was a blaze of light, that's all I saw in my vision. I feel like something was dragging. Oh, it has been torn, the young man told me it wasn't!

DOLLY. Say, who is he?

VEE. I don't know who he is, but I think he's all right, though. He told me he'd been saved, doesn't smoke, doesn't drink. His parents are dead, both of them, but he's got an uncle who's a Catholic priest and he says he stayed six years—I mean his uncle—in some leper colony on a South Sea Island without ever catching any sign of disease. Isn't that wonderful though?

DOLLY. Huh.

BEULAH. What's he doing here?

VEE. Says he's exploring the world an' ev'rything in it.

DOLLY. Laudamighty!

VEE. He come to the lockup las' night an' ast for a bed, but he couldn't stay in it, though, the bars made him nervous.

DOLLY. So what did you do with him then?

VEE. What do you mean? I was alone in the house so I give him a blanket; he went out to sleep in his car.

DOLLY. Sounds like a peculiar person.

BEULAH. Yeah.

VEE. Oh, no, he just isn't a type that you are used to seeing. I'm going to speak a good word for him to Myra, she said she might be needing some help around here.

> *Val appears in the front door. He is about twenty-five years old. He has a fresh and primitive quality, a virile grace and freedom of body, and a strong physical appeal.*

Come right on in, Mr. Xavier.

VAL. What shall I do with this here?

VEE. Jus' give me the sherbet. I thought Mr. Torrance might need somethin' light an' digestible so I brought sherbet.

BEULAH. What flavuh is it? Pineapple?

VEE. Pineapple.

BEULAH. Oh, goody, I love pineapple. Don't you-all?

Vee hands the napkin-wrapped bowl to Beulah.

VEE. Mr. Xavier, I was just telling these ladies about your uncle that went to live with the lepers. Some people are doubtful about the power of faith but there's an example I think should convince anybody.

BEULAH. Isn't it, though? Let's put this right in the Frigidaire before it stahts t' melt. *(Gives bowl to Dolly.)*

DOLLY. *(Lifting the napkin.)* I'm afraid you're locking the stable after the hause is gone.

BEULAH. Wh-at? Is it melted awready?

DOLLY. Reduced to juice! *(Gives bowl to Beulah.)*

BEULAH. Oh foot!—Well, let's put it in anyhow, it might thicken up.

VEE. Where is the Frigidaire?

BEULAH. It's in the back.

> *The three women go back through the archway. Sandra is left with Val. She laughs in her throat and leans provocatively back. Val stares at her with a touch of antagonism. This challenging silence continues for a marked pause. Then Sandra laughs again, somewhat louder.*

VAL. *(Sharply.)* Is something amusing you, lady?

SANDRA. *(Drawling.)* Yes, very much. I think it's that jacket you're wearing. What stuff is it made of?

VAL. Snakeskin.

SANDRA. *(With a disgusted grimace.)* Ouuu!

VAL. I didn't ask your opinion.

SANDRA. I didn't express one, did I?

VAL. Yeah. You said "Ouuu!" *(Mocks her grimace.)*

SANDRA. You know what that was? It was fascinated revulsion.

> *She goes into the confectionery and starts the jukebox. It plays "Bobby McGee."*[*]

Would you like to dance?

VAL. I don't know how to dance.

SANDRA. I'd love to teach you. Would you like to go out jooking some night?

VAL. Jooking? What's that?

SANDRA. That's where you get in a car and drink a little and drive a little and dance a little. Then you drink a little more and drive a little more and dance a little more. Then you stop dancing and just drink and drive. Then you stop driving and you just drink. And then, finally, you stop drinking.

VAL. Then what do you do?

SANDRA. That depends entirely on who you happen to be out jooking with. If you're out with me, and you're sufficiently attractive, you nearly always wind up on Cypress Hill.

VAL. What's that?

SANDRA. That's the graveyard, honey. It's situated, appropriately enough, on the highest point of land in Two River County, a beautiful windy bluff just west of the Sunflower River.

VAL. Why do you go out there?

SANDRA. Because dead people give such good advice.

VAL. What advice do they give?

SANDRA. Just one word—*live!*

> *Beulah rushes in with a bowl of something.*

Live! Live! Live!

BEULAH. You're going to stay fo' the pahty, Mr.…?

VAL. Xavier.

BEULAH. I know some Seviers in Blue Mountain. Any relation?

VAL. Spelt with an "S" or an "X"?

BEULAH. An "S," I believe.

---

[*] See Note on Songs and Recordings at the back of this volume.

VAL. No relation.

BEULAH. *(Sympathetically.)* Awwww.

>*She rushes back out.*

SANDRA. I have a great aunt who's laid away on Cypress Hill. Her name was Cassandra, the same as mine is. She loved to drink, so I always empty my bottles on her grave. She finally got so she just lay on the bed and drank and drank all night and all day. They asked her if she didn't get tired of it. She said, "No, I never get bored. I have moving pictures on my ceiling. They go on all the time, continuous performance. I'm the main actress," she said, "and I do the most mah-velous things!" That was Cassandra the second. I'm the third. The first was a little Greek girl who slept in the shrine of Apollo. Her ears were snake-bitten, like mine, so that she could understand the secret language of the birds. You know what they told her, Snakeskin? They contradicted everything that she'd been told before. They said it was all stuff an' nonsense, a pack of lies. They advised her to drive her car as fast as she wanted to drive it, to dance like she wanted to dance. "Get drunk," they said, "raise hell at Moon Lake casino, do bumps an' wiggle your fanny!"

>*Vee Talbott enters; she stops short with an outraged look.*
>*Sandra laughs and extends a pack of cigarettes toward Val.*

VEE. Mr. Xavier don't smoke.

>*Vee sets the potato chips down and goes out.*

DOLLY. *(Rushing through with Beulah.)* Mr. Xavier, if you're looking for work, you might drop in on my husband, Pee Wee Bland. He runs that cotton gin right over the road there.

BEULAH. The marguerites! I smell them burning!

>*She runs out.*

SANDRA. How did you happen to come to this dark, wild river country of ours?

VAL. A broken axle stopped me here last night.

SANDRA. You'd better mend it quick and move along.

VAL. Why's that?

SANDRA. Why? Why? Don't you know what those women are

suffering from: Sexual Malnutrition! They look at you with eyes that scream "Eureka!" You know what they say about me, I'm corrupt.

VAL. If you don't want to be talked about, why do you wear make-up like that? Why do you…

SANDRA. To show off. I'm an exhibitionist. I want to be noticed, seen, heard, felt. I want them to know I'm alive.

> *She fires two shots.*

Don't you want them to know you're alive?

> *She fires twice again. Val takes the gun from her.*

VAL. I want to live. I don't care if they know I'm alive or not!

> *There are screams as the Temple Sisters come in from upstairs, Blanch falls and hurts her ankle, Vee and Beulah enter and Dolly from outside.*

DOLLY. What are you doing? Oh, God, in my condition! I…

BEULAH. Sandra, for the love of…

BLANCH. I've broke my leg in two!

EVA. She's broke her laig!

DOLLY. Oh she has not! Sandra, what on earth did you fire that damn thing for?

SANDRA. I took a pot shot at a buzzard!

BEULAH. A what?

> *Myra enters store from front door.*

MYRA. What in God's name has been going on here? Who fired those shots out the door?

> *She sees Val with the revolver.*

You!

VAL. *(Slowly smiling.)* No ma'am, it wasn't me. It was this young lady here.

SANDRA. Yes, I fired it, darling.

MYRA. What at?

SANDRA. A bird of ill omen was circling over the store.

MYRA. Yea? One of those imaginary things that people see in a certain condition. Hello, Beulah, Dolly. *(Flings off her hat.)* I'm evermore tired. I've never had such a trip. Jabe took a bad spell on the train. How are yuh, Vee. Blanch Temple, what are you sitting on the floor faw?

EVA. She took a spill on the stairs when Sandra Whiteside fired the shots!

MYRA. On the stairs? You two were upstairs, were you?

EVA. Yes, we were straightening things up a little…

MYRA. *(Quickly.)* I see. An investigation?

EVA. Yes. I mean…

BLANCH. No, no, no! We wanted to see that ev'rything was in order. I've got such awful weak ankles, I'm always tripping and falling. An' I've got to march in church with the choir if I got to go on crutches.

> *She rises painfully with Beulah's and Eva's assistance. Jabe enters helped by Pee Wee and Talbott.*

EVA. Cousin Jabe is here.

DOLLY. Jabe, welcome home. Look at the color he's got in his face.

BEULAH. Looks like he's been to Miami and got a Florida suntan!

JABE. I ain't been out in no sun and if you all excuse me I'm going to do my celebratin' in bed, 'cause I'm all worn out.

> *He climbs to his room.*

MYRA. Oh, look what you all have done, that beautiful table! Candles an' ev'rything sweet that goes to make a nice party! Some of your lovely floating island, Beulah? Sweet! The spirit is willing but the flesh is completely exhausted.

> *A Negro enters, crosses to Myra carrying a tower of pastel-colored hatboxes and a big gay placard reading "Welcome Sweet Springtime."*

Oh, Loon, bring me those cards. Welcome sweet springtime! I've bought a pile of spring hats.

> *She extricates one of the cards.*

This one here is the nicest—"In the spring, a young maid's fancy lightly turns to new chapeaux."

BEULAH. *(Reading the rest of it.)* "Mary Lou and Jane and Frances wear new hats to please their beaux!"

DOLLY. Oh, that's perfectly dahling. It seems so eahly, though, to think about spring.

EVA. I don't know. Somebody tole me that carps have been seen in Yazoo Pass. That always indicates that flood season's 'bout to start.

>   *All chatter.*

BLANCH. Myra…

MYRA. Yes?

BLANCH. I don't suppose you feel like talkin' about it right now, but I do hope Jabe's operation was completely successful.

MYRA. No.

BLANCH. It wasn't?

>   *All the women stare greedily at Myra.*

MYRA. No. It *wasn't.*

BLANCH. Oh!

EVA. My! My!

BEULAH. I'm so sorry to hear it.

DOLLY. If there's anything I can do… I—?

>   *Jabe is heard knocking on the ceiling from his room above. Myra's face becomes suddenly listless and tired.*

EVA. What's that knocking upstairs?

MYRA. Jabe.

TALBOTT. *(Calling from above.)* Myra, Jabe wants you.

MYRA. Excuse me, I'll have to go up.

>   *She crosses wearily toward the stairs, her hat dangling from one hand, pauses before the "Welcome Sweet Springtime" sign, with its bluebirds, flutes, and gilded scrolls and cherubim, gravely lifts it and places it in a higher position.*

Dolly, look at this hat! I think it must have been created just for you!

>   *She smiles and goes on upstairs.*

SANDRA. *(Who has engaged Val in low conversation since Myra's entrance.)* Speaking of knocks, I've got one in my engine. It goes knock knock, and I say "Who's there?" A very mysterious noise. I can't decide whether I'm in communication with one of my dead ancestors or whether the carburetor or something is just about to drop out an' leave me stranded, probably at midnight in the middle of some lonesome black forest!

> *She smiles at Val.*

I don't suppose you'd have any knowledge of mechanics?

VAL. I dunno. I might.

> *Dolly is trying on the hat but is watchful of this exchange— also the other women who are opening hatboxes.*

SANDRA. Would you be willing to undertake a kind of exploratory operation on it?

VAL. Well, I might if it didn't take too long.

SANDRA. *(Drawling.)* Oh, with your expert knowledge it shouldn't take lo-ong at-all!

DOLLY. *(Giggles.)* This hat! Isn't it the strangest thing?

BEULAH. Them things on the brim—what are they—carrots an' peas? I think they'd be much better *creamed*—with chicken croquettes!

> *Val has slid slowly off the counter. He moves past Sandra and the secret looks of the women, toward the door.*

VEE. Mr. Xavier…

> *She crosses as if to stop him but Val and Sandra have already disappeared.*

Oh, I was going to ask Myra if she would give him a job.

BEULAH. Well …

DOLLY. It looks like he's *got* one now!

EVA. What did she say? A knock…?

BLANCH. In her engine! *(Innocently.)* Whatever that is.

DOLLY. *(With a peal of laughter.)* Did you *evuh* see such a puh-faum-ance! *Nevuh* in all my…

BEULAH. Bawn days? *Neither* did I! You see how she looked at the boy? An' the tone of huh voice. Corrupt? Absolutely—de-*grad-ed*!

VEE. *(Who has been silently brooding over the situation.)* I certainly hope she doesn't get him to drink.

DOLLY. Vee, honey, you might as well face it, this is one candidate fo' salvation that you have *lost* to the opposition!

VEE. I don't believe it. He told me that he'd been saved already.

She fixes her resentment on Dolly.

If some of the older women in Two River County would set a better example there'd be more justice in their talk about girls!

DOLLY. *(With asperity.)* What do you mean by that remark?

VEE. I mean that people who give drinkin' pahties an' get so drunk they don't know which is *their husband* an' which is somebody else's an' people who serve on the altar guild an' still play cards on Sundays…

DOLLY. Just stop right there! Now I've discovered the source of that dirty gossip!

VEE. I'm only repeating what I've been told by others! I certainly never have been entertained at such affairs as that!

DOLLY. No, an' you never will be; you're a public killjoy, a professional hypocrite!

BEULAH. Dolly!

DOLLY. She spends her time refawming tramps that her husband puts in the *lockup*! Bring them here in Myra's store an' tries to get them jobs here when God knows what kind of vicious ideas they've probably got in their heads!

VEE. I try to build up characters! You an' your drinkin' pahties are only concerned with tearin' characters down! I'm goin' upstairs with Myra.

Vee goes out.

DOLLY. Well, you know what brought on that tantrum? She's jealous of Sandra Whiteside's running off with that strange boy. She hasn't lived as a natural wife for ten years or more *(To Eva.)* so her husband has got to pick up with some bright-skinned nigger.

BEULAH. Oh, Dolly, you're awful. Sometimes I think you ought to wear a backhouse on your haid instead of a hat.

DOLLY. I've got no earthly patience with that sort of hypocriticism. Beulah, let's put all this perishable stuff in the Frigidaire and get out of here. I've never been so thoroughly disgusted.

BEULAH. Oh, my Lawd!

EVA. Both of those two women are as common as dirt.

BLANCH. Dolly's folks in Blue Mountain are nothin' at all but the poorest kind of white trash. Why, Lollie Tucker told me the old man sits on the porch with his shoes off drinkin' beer out of a bucket! Nobody wants these marguerites.

> *She goes to the hardware counter and gets her bag.*

Let's take 'em, huh?

EVA. *(Looking at the flowers.)* I was just wondering what we'd use to decorate the altar with tomorrow. The bishop adjutant's comin'. As far's I know nobody's offered flowers. We can give Myra credit in the parish notes.

BLANCH. Put the olive-nut sandwiches in here with the marguerites. Be careful you tote them so they won't get squashed.

EVA. They'll come in very nicely for the bishop's tea.

> *Dolly and Beulah reenter from the back.*

DOLLY. We still have time to make the second show.

> *Dolly and Beulah go out quickly together.*

EVA. *(When they are out.)* Sits on the po'ch with his shoes off?

BLANCH. Yes! Drinkin' *beer* from a *bucket*!

> *Eva and Blanch go out. The sheriff comes downstairs, grunting and puffing, followed by Pee Wee.*

PEE WEE. Took one dose at noon. When that didn't work, I took a double one about five o'clock. Jabe sure looks bad.

TALBOTT. Looks no better 'n' no worse 'n he always looked, but if what they say is correct, he'll more'n likely go under before the cotton comes up! See that there? *(Indicates his bandaged knuckle.)* Broke my knuckle! Never hit a bucktooth nigger in the mouf! That's *the moral of it.*

> *Pee Wee laughs.*

Oh, Vee! …Them fool wimmin got in a ruckus down here, I don't know what it's about.

> *Vee comes downstairs.*

VEE. Hush that bawling will yuh! I wanted to speak with Myra about that young man who needs work but I couldn't in front of Jabe. He thinks he's gonna be able to go back to work himself.

TALBOTT. Well, come awn here, quit foolin'!

VEE. I think I ought to wait till that young man gets back.

TALBOTT. Mama, you come awn. Aw else stay here, an' *walk* when you git ready.

> *He strides out after Pee Wee. The car engine roars. Vee looks troubled and follows them slowly out. There is a slight pause. The Conjure Man enters from the confectionery. He looks about him and laughs with a gentle, quiet laughter at something secret, opens the soft-drink cooler and takes a Coke out. He laughs again, softly, secretly, and goes out the front door of the store, leaving the door open. A hound bays in the distance. After a moment Val comes back in, and shuts the door behind him. He goes to the table, picks up a paper napkin and scrubs lipstick off his mouth. He settles himself on the counter. After a moment or two Myra comes downstairs bearing an oil lamp. She has on a cheap Japanese kimono of shiny black satin with large scarlet poppies on it. She appears to be very distraught and doesn't notice Val. She crosses directly to the phone and turns the crank.*

MYRA. Get me the drugstore, please. Mr. Dubinsky? This is Myra Torrance. Were you asleep? I'm sorry. I'm in a bad situation. I left my Luminal tablets in the Memphis hotel and I can't sleep without them. …I know your store's closed up. So's mine. I know the lights are out, they're out over here. But you don't need a thousand-watt bulb to put a few Luminal tablets in a little cardboard box or paper bag. …Now look here, Mr. Dubinsky, if you want to keep my trade, you send your nigger right over with that box of tablets. Gone? Then bring 'em yourself! I'm absolutely desperate from lack of sleep. My nerves are all on edge. If I don't get a good sleep tonight, I'll go all to pieces. I've got a sick man to take care of. …Yes, I just brought him home from the Memphis hospital. The operation was not at all successful. Will you do that? I'll be very much obliged. Thank you, Mr. Dubinsky. Excuse me for speaking so sharply. Thank you, Mr. Dubinsky. I appreciate that, Mr. Dubinsky. Good-bye, Mr. Dubinsky.

Oh, oh, oh, I wish I was dead—dead—dead.

VAL. *(Quietly.)* No, you don't, Mrs. Torrance.

MYRA. My God!

VAL. I didn't mean to scare you.

MYRA. *What is this?* What are you still doing here? Who *are you?* My God, you got eyes that shine in the dark like a dog's. Get out or I'll call for the sheriff!

VAL. Lady…

MYRA. Well?

VAL. I've been to the sheriff's already.

MYRA. Aw. Escaped from the lockup?

VAL. Naw. The sheriff's wife took me in there last night.

MYRA. She did, uh?

VAL. She give me a night's flop there but I didn't stay.

MYRA. Naw?

VAL. It made me uneasy being locked up. I got to have space around me.

MYRA. Look here, that's interesting, but this store's closed and I'll thank you to please get out. I've got a sick man upstairs that requires a lot of attention. If you're hungry…

VAL. I'm not.

MYRA. There's lots of fancy stuff they put in the Frigidaire, you might as well eat it, I can't.

VAL. No, thanks, but I'd be mighty obliged if you would give me a job.

MYRA. There's no work here.

VAL. Excuse the contradiction but there is. Mizz Talbott told me so.

MYRA. Vee Talbott? I'll thank her to let me decide such things for myself. I'm in the mercantile business, she's a painter of very peculiar pictures she calls the Apostles but look like men around town. She took you in, did she? Well!

VAL. Whatever it is you're suggesting is incorrect. I've met one bitch in this town but it wasn't her.

MYRA. *(Furiously.)* How—how—*dare* you say that!

VAL. It wasn't you neither, ma'am! It was one that picked me up in here before you come in. Said she had engine trouble and would I fix it. She took me for a stud—and I slapped her face!

MYRA. You *what*?

VAL. I said I slapped her face. She wasn't a bad piece neither but I didn't like the way she went about it, like she was something special and I was trash!

MYRA. You… Cassandra Whiteside? *Slapped?*

> *She bursts into wild laughter.*

I've never heard anything so beautiful in all my life! Have a drink and get out; I've got to go up.

VAL. *(Stubbornly.)* You'll need help here with your husband sick upstairs.

MYRA. You think so, uh? Well, if I do it'll have to be local help. I couldn't hire no stranger. 'Specially one that slapped the face of the richest girl in the Mississippi Delta.

> *She laughs again.*

You had sales experience?

VAL. I've had all kinds of experience.

MYRA. That's not what I ast you. I ast you if you've had experience in the mercantile line. I want to know if you would be able to sell?

VAL. Sell?

MYRA. Yes!

VAL. Lots in hell to preachers!

MYRA. I guess you got character ref'rence?

VAL. Sure.

MYRA. Where was the last place you worked?

VAL. Garage in Oakley.

MYRA. Tennessee?

VAL. Yeah.

MYRA. Grease monkey, was you?

VAL. *(Stiffly.)* I wouldn't call myself that.

MYRA. Excuse me. Why did you quit that job?

VAL. If I told you, you'd think I was crazy.

MYRA. I think ev'rybody is crazy, including myself. Why did you quit it?

VAL. The place next door burnt down.

MYRA. What's that got to do with it?

VAL. I don't like fire. I dreamed about it three nights straight so I quit. I was burnt as a kid and ever since then it's been something I can't forget. *(Offers her a paper.)* Here's a letter he wrote.

MYRA. Who?

VAL. Garage manager.

MYRA. *(Reading aloud.)* "This here boy's peculiar but he sure does work real hard and he's honest as daylight." What does he mean "peculiar"?

VAL. Unusual is what he means.

MYRA. Why don't he say unusual?

VAL. He's not exactly an expert in the use of the language.

MYRA. Oh, but you are?

VAL. You ever seen a coal miner's cap?

> *Myra shakes her head.*

I wore one once when I was mining in the Red Hills of Alabama. It had a little lamp in front so you could see what your pick was digging into. Well—I'm still digging.

MYRA. Digging?

VAL. I don't claim to know very much, but I am writing a *book*.

MYRA. What's your book about?

VAL. Life.

MYRA. Sorry, but I can't use you.

VAL. Why not?

MYRA. Other people ain't as charitable as that garage manager is.

They wouldn't say "peculiar," they'd say "nuts!" Also your appearance is much against you.

VAL. What's wrong with that.

MYRA. I don't know exactly. If you're hungry, eat. But otherwise…

> *She is interrupted by knocking on the ceiling.*

Otherwise…get out. I'm too bone-tired to carry on conversation.

VAL. If you'll excuse me for telling you so, you're just about the rudest talking woman I've ever met.

MYRA. Yes, I'm mean inside. You heard me cussing when I come downstairs? Inside I cuss like that all the time. I hate ev'rybody; I wish this town would be bombarded tomorrow and everyone daid. Because—

VAL. Because?

MYRA. I got to live in it when I'd rather be daid in it—an' buried. What I meant about your appearance is you're too good-looking. Can you read shoe sizes?

VAL. Yeah.

MYRA. What does 75 David mean?

> *Val is stymied.*

You see how you lie? You lie like a dawg in summer!

> *She laughs, not unkindly.*

75 means 7 1/2 in length and David means D wide. For flat-footed wimmin. You would either scare trade out of this store completely or else you'd bring it in so thick the floor would collapse. I can't decide which it would be.

VAL. I'd bring it in, lady. (*Rubs knuckles.*)

MYRA. Gosh—

> *There is a knock at the front door. Myra crosses to it.*

A new floor would be an awful expense!

> *She opens the door and steps outside.*

Thank you, Mr. Dubinsky. (*Coming back in.*) That was the sandman with my Luminal tablets. Suppose you—

VAL. Huh?

MYRA. Suppose you try to sell me a pair of white kid pumps out
of that new stock there. Imagine me a customer hard to please and
you the clerk. Go on. …Naw, them over there is Red Goose shoes
for kiddies. Them're men's shoes. Growing girls', misses'. Them on
the end of the shelves are women's; sizes range down from the top.

He pulls out a pair.

You call them kid? That's suede, young man; 'snot a pump, neither,
's a blucher oxford; I don't believe you've ever tried to sell a thing in
your life. Go on, roll your hoop, you're worse than useless to me!
(As he moves slowly toward the door, Myra says softly:) Sure you're
not hungry? You're walking kind of unsteady.

VAL. What's that to you? I've got dog's eyes—you don't like me!

MYRA. I didn't say that.

VAL. I can't read shoe sizes. I don't know suede from kid. You can't
use me; I'm worse than useless! What does it matter whether I'm
hungry or not?

He shakes with fury.

MYRA. *(Very softly, gently, with a slight mournful, tender shake of
her head.)* Lawd, child, come back in the mawning and I'll give you
a job.

VAL. God, I—! Lady, you—!

MYRA. *(Laughing a little.)* God you an' lady me, huh. I think you
are kind of exaggerating a little in both cases.

*They laugh. She blows out one of the candles, leaving two
lighted.*

You never have any trouble getting to sleep?

VAL. No. I know how to relax.

MYRA. How do you relax?

VAL. Imagine yourself a loose piece of string.

MYRA. A loose piece of string. That's lovely! I'm a loose piece of
string.

> *There is a knock on the ceiling.*

VAL. What's that knocking upstairs?

MYRA. Jabe.

> *She averts her face.*

VAL. Who?

MYRA. My husband.

VAL. It scared me for a minute.

MYRA. Why?

VAL. Clump. Clump. Clump. Sounds like a skeleton walking around upstairs.

MYRA. Maybe you're gifted with too much imagination.

VAL. Uh-huh. That's always been one of my biggest troubles.

> *The candles gutter out. A dog is heard baying in the distance; the sound has a peculiar, passionate clarity.*

MYRA. *(Softly.)* Hear that houn' dawg? …He's bayin' at th' moon. …Sky's cleared off? …Yes, it's clean as a whistle. …Isn't that nice?

VAL. *(Hoarsely.)* Yes, ma'am.

MYRA. Well…

> *It grows rapidly darker as they stand hesitantly apart, looking at each other. Myra turns slowly back toward the stairs.*

Well…the door locks itself when you slam it. Good night.

VAL. *(Speaking in a low, hoarse whisper.)* G'night.

> *She starts up the stairs, slowly. He opens the door. Once more the dog is heard baying. They both stop short as though caught by the magic of the sound and face each other again from the stairway and the door. Val speaks again, still more hoarsely.*

G'night.

MYRA. *(In a whisper.)* Good night.

CURTAIN

ACT TWO

Scene 1

It is about a week later. Val is seated on the counter of the store leaning dreamily against a shelf. In his hand is a pencil and a shoebox lid. He is raptly composing an idyllic passage in his book. The jukebox is playing as he speaks aloud. Myra appears in the confectionery archway with a couple of boxes. She overhears his soliloquy and stops short to listen.

VAL. Day used to come up slow through the long white curtains.

MYRA. Val!

> *Val starts.*

Who are you talking to?

VAL. Myself, I suppose.

MYRA. Isn't that kind of peculiar, talking to yourself?

VAL. No, ma'am. That's just a habit that lonesome people get into.

MYRA. Please don't do it when anyone's in the store. I don't want it spread around town that a lunatic's been employed here. That sunshine's *terrific*—you better let down the awnings.

> *Val moves slowly from the counter.*

Slew-foot!

VAL. Huh?

MYRA. Slew-foot, slew-foot! You walk like you're on flypapers! Pick up your feet when you walk and get a *move* on!

> *Val laughs and saunters leisurely out the door.*

Talks to himself, writing poems on shoeboxes! What a mess.

> *She stares through the window as Val lowers the awning. Three young girls follow Val as he comes back in.*

EDNA MAE. Hello!

VAL. *(Amiably.)* Hello there.

EDNA MAE. Jane wants to look at some kickies.

JANE. *(Giggling.)* No—you do.

SHERRI-LEE. I'd like to try on some. Can you dance in kickies?

VAL. Sure you can dance in kickies. Sit down there. Let's measure your little foot.

EDNA MAE. *(Beating her to the chair.)* Me first, me first.

VAL. Okay. First come, first serve.

> *He pulls her shoe off. She giggles spasmodically.*

Five and one half, Bennie.

> *He goes to the shelf.*

EDNA MAE. Isn't he *cute?*

JANE. Say, do you dance?

> *Val laughs.*

SHERRI-LEE. Would you like to go out jooking?

MYRA. Val! I'll wait on these girls. You take these empty boxes out of here.

> *As soon as Val leaves, the girls giggle and run out of the store. Myra looks very annoyed as Eva Temple enters.*

EVA. Mr. Xa-*vier?*

MYRA. *(Sharply.)* Our popular young shoe clerk is in the basement. What do you want?

EVA. A pair of bedroom slippers.

MYRA. Sit down and I'll show you some.

EVA. I'll wait till Mr. Xavier comes back upstairs. He seems to understand my feet so well. How's Cousin Jabe this mawning?

MYRA. Just the same.

EVA. Dear me—

> *Val reappears.*

Mr. Xa-*vier!*

VAL. How are you this mawning?

EVA. I seem to be comin' down with th' most abominable earache.

MYRA. *(Sympathetically.)* Aww! Let me give you a little laudanum faw it.

EVA. No, thanks. I put some in already. I think Birdie Wilson was partially responsible faw it.

VAL. Why? Is earache contagious?

EVA. No, but Birdie was singing right next to me at choir practice, which did it absolutely no good.

> *She titters a little.*

What'm I sittin' here faw?

VAL. T' look at some shoes.

EVA. Aw. Well, I guess I might. Haven't you all noticed about Birdie? Her voice always cracks on that *Te Deum*. She can hit "A" pretty good but she always flats on "B." You'd think she'd have better sense than to even attempt to make "C" because it's completely out of her range, but I'll say this for Birdie, she's got the courage of her convictions.

VAL. These are the new wine shades.

EVA. Oh! Pretty! Yes, she goes right on up there and I'm telling you all, it's a perfect imitation of the Cannonball Express. *(Giggles.)* Oh, my goodness, these *pinch*!

VAL. Do they?

EVA. They certainly do. *(Giggles archly.)*

VAL. Well, let's try a David on that.

EVA. What's David?

VAL. Next size broader!

EVA. Oh, my goodness, no! There must be some mistake!

VAL. *(Climbing the shelf ladder.)* Don't you know what a broad foot's a sign of, Miss Temple? Imagination! And also of…

EVA. Of *what*?

> *Cassandra Whiteside enters the front door.*

MYRA. Hello, Sandra!

SANDRA. Hello, Myra. I just drove home from New Awleuns fo' the Delta Planters' Cotillion. And do you know I neglected to bring a single decent pair of evenin' slippers back with me.

MYRA. Oh, honey, we don't keep evenin' slippers in stock, we don't get any calls fo' them here.

SANDRA. *(Noticing Val.)* I didn't suppose you would.

MYRA. Oh, wait! Val, reach me down that old Queen Quality box up there!

Dolly and Beulah enter.

BEULAH. Well, it is exasperating to have your table broke up at the very last… *Sandra!*

DOLLY. Sandra Whiteside! I thought you were gonna stay in New Awleuns till after Mardi Gras.

SANDRA. I just drove home for the Delta Planters' Cotillion.

MYRA. *(Wistfully.)* How is Mardi Gras this yeah?

SANDRA. As mahvelously mad as usual. If I were refawming the world I'd make it last forever.

MYRA. I went to it once a long, long time ago. I remembuh they danced in the streets.

SANDRA. They do ev'rything in the streets!

MYRA. I was just fourteen. Something wonderful happened.

SANDRA. What was it?

MYRA. A boy in a Pierrot suit.

SANDRA. How lovely! What did he do?

MYRA. Caught me around the waist, whirled me till I was dizzy—then kissed me and—*disappeared!*

SANDRA. Disappeared?

MYRA. Completely. In the crowd. The music stopped. I ran straight back to my room and lay on the bed an' stared an' stared at a big yellow spot on the ceiling.

SANDRA. Oh, my Lawd, how tragic.

MYRA. It *was. (Smiles.)*

SANDRA. Your first heartbreak!

MYRA. Uh-huh. *(Laughs.)*

VAL. *(Bringing a shoebox.)* This one?

MYRA. *Yes, that's it. (To Sandra.)* I hope you're not superstitious!

SANDRA. *(Lighting a cigarette.)* Why?

MYRA. Because this box contains some silver and white satin slippers that were intended for Rosemary Wildberger…

DOLLY. Rosemary!

BEULAH. Wildberger!

MYRA. …To wear at her wedding exactly three years ago this Valentine's Day.

> *She lifts one of the slippers.*

She had such a tiny foot.

BEULAH. Such a tiny, delicate girl. Rosemary…

DOLLY. Wildberger!

SANDRA. *(Laughing lightly.)* Well, what happened? Did she fall dead at the altar?

BEULAH. Oh, no.

DOLLY. Worse than that!

BEULAH. Much worse. The man stood her up.

MYRA. Where did Rosemary go, does anyone know?

BEULAH. Some people say she went crazy an' some people say she went to Cincinnati to study voice.

SANDRA. *(Carelessly.)* Which was it?

EVA. *(Piping up resentfully, having been ignored.)* Neither. She went into Chinese missionary work.

DOLLY. *(Sarcastically.)* Trust Eva Temple to have complete information.

BEULAH. Oh, yes.

SANDRA. And these are the fabulous Rosemary's little silver and white wedding slippers. How lovely.

MYRA. I ordered 'em from St. Louis for her but, of course, I never had the heart to mention them to her parents after she disappeared. What size do you wear, honey?

SANDRA. Four, triple A.

MYRA. Gracious. These are four B. Val, see how they fit Miss Whiteside. *(Turns to Dolly.)* Oh, Dolly, I wanted you to see this;

soon as I unpacked it I had vision of you!

>   *She removes an outlandish red dress with brass trimming from the racks; it looks like a bareback rider's outfit.*

DOLLY. *(Rushing to it.)* Oh, my God, ain't it lovely! But you know, honey, I won't be able to wear anything one-piece this spring.

MYRA. Really?

DOLLY. Oh, for the usual reason. Y'know there's absolutely no justice in nature. I mean the way she ties some women down while others can run hog wild. Look at Myra, for instance. Not one kid an' me turning out the seventh.

MYRA. *(Averting her face.)* Bring your measurements—I'll order you some maternity garments from Memphis.

DOLLY. Measurements? Fifteen square yards. How long'll it take?

MYRA. Probably two or three weeks.

>   *Dolly shrieks and throws up her hands.*

Can't you wait that long?

DOLLY. I can, but my figure can't.

>   *Blanch Temple enters, and trips over the rubber mat at the door. She utters a shrill cry.*

EVA. *(Jumping up.)* Blanch, that might have *thrown* you!

MYRA. Val, you must tack that down.

VAL. Get the nigger to do it.

BLANCH. My ankle is twisted. I can't even step on that foot.

EVA. Oh, my Lawd, she'll have to have it treated again. Cost us eight or ten dollars. I simply can't pay for these shoes.

MYRA. All right, you don't have to, Eva, we'll just call it square. Val! Wrap these up for Miss Temple. *(Turns to Sandra.)* How did they fit?

>   *Val picks up the shoes and goes to the cash register.*

SANDRA. I couldn't wear them. Let me see a pair of plain white pumps.

MYRA. Surely.

DOLLY. We must be goin', Beulah, bye, bye, you all.

Dolly and Beulah go out.

BEULAH. *(Her voice is heard offstage.)* I just been thinkin'. Lulu Belle don't play contract at all. She just plays auction.

MYRA. Hurry back!

She gets some other shoes down; sits on the stool; opens the box for Sandra.

BLANCH. *(Peeking among the valentines on the counter.)* Here's where she must've bought it 'cause here's another just like it.

VAL. What's that?

BLANCH. Somebody sent us a comic valentine. It wasn't funny at all, it was simply malicious. Old maids. There's no such thing as an old maid anymore.

EVA. No, they're bachelor girls.

VAL. *(Suppressing a smile.)* Here's your shoes, Miss Temple.

EVA. Oh, thanks, aw'fly. Miss DeQuincy was telling me you'd been to Yellowstone Park.

VAL. I've traveled all over, not only Yellowstone Park, but Yosemite, Gran' Canyon…

BLANCH. How marvelous. Why don't we get him to give us a little descriptive talk at our next auxiliary meeting?

EVA. Oh, would you do that, Mr…

VAL. Xavier.

EVA. Mr. Xavier. You won't fo'get the meeting?

BLANCH. It's Saturday at four fifteen.

MYRA. Val couldn't take the time off. We're too rushed on Saturday afternoon.

EVA. Aw, what a shame.

BLANCH. Goodbye, Mr. Xavier.

They go out.

SANDRA. Aren't they delightful. The little white doves of the Lord. *(With a sidelong glance at Val.)* Do you suppose I'll get like that if I remain a virgin?

MYRA. Well, I don't believe I'd worry about it, Sandra.

Jabe knocks overhead.

SANDRA. Ouuu! What's that noise?

MYRA. Jabe's knocking. *(Her faces darkens.)*

SANDRA. Oh.

MYRA. I'll have to run up for a minute.

She goes quickly upstairs.

SANDRA. *(Lighting a cigarette, with a quizzical look at Val.)* I didn't come in here for evening slippers.

VAL. No. I figured you didn't.

SANDRA. I didn't come home for the Delta Planters' Cotillion. I came back here to see you. I haven't been able to get you off my mind. I woke up thinking about you last night in the Hotel Monteleone. I went downstairs to the bar at three o'clock in the morning. I thought I might forget if I got drunk. They must've poured my whiskey out of the wrong bottle, though. At half past three I was on the highway, headed back to Two Rivers—seventy, eighty, ninety miles an hour— scared that you'd be gone before I got here. What do you think about that?

VAL. I think you'd better go back to the Mardi Gras.

SANDRA. You don't like me very much, do you?

VAL. I want to keep this job. Every place I've gone to it's been some woman I finally had to leave on account of.

SANDRA. I believe that. You're the center of much discussion in Two River County—among the women. That snakeskin jacket, those eyes; that special technique you use in fitting on shoes.

VAL. I don't use any special technique.

SANDRA. Maybe they just imagine that you do. I can understand why. You're beautiful, you're wild. I have a feeling we'll come together some night.

VAL. Yeah?

SANDRA. *(Rhapsodically.)* In the dark of the moon, beside a broken fence rail in some big rolling meadow.

Val turns away.

We won't even say hello.

VAL. Let's quit this!

SANDRA. This what?

VAL. Double talk.

SANDRA. All right.

> She removes her dark glasses and arches her body in a provocative pose. She speaks childishly.

Why did you slap me, Val?

VAL. Because.

SANDRA. Just because?

VAL. I didn't want to be interfered with by you. You think I've got a sign "Male at Stud" hung on me?

SANDRA. Yes, I think you have. Nobody could possibly make a mistake about it.

VAL. You made a mistake about it. I'm not in your class. I'm the kind of fellow you get to wash your car or chop the cotton. That night you drove me up to Cypress Hill, I wasn't nothing to you. It was like you had hired me to give you a little amusement.

SANDRA. That's what you thought? You were wrong about that. I felt a resemblance between us.

VAL. There's none that I know of, lady.

SANDRA. You must be blind. You—savage. And me—aristocrat. Both of us things whose license has been revoked in the civilized world. Both of us equally damned and for the same good reason. Because we both want freedom. Of course, I knew you were really better than me. A whole lot better. I'm rotten. Neurotic. Our blood's gone bad from too much interbreeding. They've set up the guillotine, not in the Place de Concorde, but here, inside our own bodies!

VAL. Double talk, smart double talk.

SANDRA. No. Look at my wrists. They're too thin. You could snap them like twigs. You can see through my skin. It's transparent like tissue paper. I'm lovely, aren't I? But I'm not any good. I wear dark glasses over my eyes because I've got secrets in them. Too much of something that makes me rather disgusting. Yes, you were right when you slapped me, Val. You should have killed me, before I kill myself. I will someday. I have an instinct for self-destruction. I'm running away from it all the time. Too fast. New Orleans, Vicksburg, Mobile. All over the God damn country with something after me every inch of the way! But the poison I've got in my blood isn't the kind that makes me fatal to kiss! Why don't you kiss me, Val?

Val moves away from her but she follows him.

Scaredy cat! *Scaredy cat!*

Val catches his breath and starts to embrace her. She suddenly jabs him in the middle with her knee and bites his hand. She laughs wildly.

There! There now! That's what I came back for! Nobody's ever slapped me and gotten away with it, Snakeskin! Goodbye!

She runs out the door.

VAL. God damn little bitch!

Myra appears on the stairway.

MYRA. What did she do?

VAL. She dared me to kiss her.

MYRA. Did you oblige her this time or did you slap her again?

VAL. I would've done it if she hadn't kicked me.

MYRA. Well, I'm glad that she kicked you. You can find some other place to do your carrying on.

VAL. I wasn't carrying on.

MYRA. You just admitted you would have if she'd let you.

She goes to the shelves.

Oh, lights of delirium, look where you put the kids!

VAL. You didn't say where to put them.

MYRA. In six days time I thought you might've caught on to where some things belong in this store.

VAL. Look here, if I was a mind reader, lady, I'd put up a tent on the commons and tell your fate by the stars at fifty cents a disaster!

MYRA. Disaster is right! I wish you'd use your noggin for something beside sweet looks at the women! Anybody with the brain of a newborn calf should know better'n to put a bunch of kids in here with—look at that, will you?

She tosses a box furiously to the floor.

Those Queen Quality evening slippers stuck in here, too. Why don't you fill up the rest of the space with cigar boxes and candy bars? Why do you wanta show so little imagination that you don't put nothing but shoes in the Shoe Department? You're writing a book? Surely you can think of some fancy new ideas like hanging dresses from the ceiling fans!

VAL. Look here, Myra.

MYRA. Since when am I Myra to you? My name is Mrs. Torrance!

VAL. You call me Val.

MYRA. That's different. I'm the employer here, you work in my store!

VAL. You mean I *worked* in your goddam store!

> *He tears off his white clerk's jacket and flings it to the floor. There is a shocked silence.*

MYRA. I was going to give you your notice tonight, anyhow.

VAL. You don't have to give it to me, I've already took it.

MYRA. Well, you can't walk out in the middle of the day like this.

VAL. Why not? I'm no help to you.

MYRA. I didn't say that…

VAL. Oh, no? Actions speak louder than words, Mrs. Torrance!

> *Myra looks at him, stunned, as he puts on his snakeskin jacket. A Negro huckster passes along the street singing "String beans, new potatoes, rutabagas."*

You are a very difficult, hardheaded woman—and much as I wanted a job I got to admit that working for you is no pleasure. When you tell me to do things, how can I understand you, the way you talk?

MYRA. The way I talk?

VAL. You talk to the *wall*. You talk to the *ceiling*. You never talk straight to *me*! You never even look in my face when you say something to me! I just have to guess what you said 'cause you talk so fast an' hard an' keep your face turned away… I've had the feeling ever since I come here that everything I do has displeased you!

MYRA. *(Averting her face.)* I didn't mean to give you that impression. As a matter of fact I was pretty well satisfied with the way you were coming along.

VAL. You certainly kept your satisfaction a secret.

MYRA. I know, I know. I'm nervous, I'm cross, I'm jumpy. *(Pathetically.)* I thought that you understood my nervous condition and made some allowance for it!

VAL. Being nervous is no excuse for acting like a nine-tailed catawampus!

MYRA. What is a nine-tailed catawampus?

VAL. I don't know. But I sure would hate to meet one.

MYRA. *(Hurt.)* Oh! How should I act with you—you carrying on with people like Sandra Whiteside—right here in the store!

VAL. So that's why you flew off the handle.

MYRA. Not just that. You know why those high school girls keep flocking in here?

VAL. Sure. To buy spring shoes.

MYRA. Spring shoes nothing! They come in here for a *thrill*!

VAL. A *what*?

MYRA. A *thrill*. You know what that is, don't you?

VAL. *(Laughing.)* Can I help it?

MYRA. Yes! You don't have to *give* them one.

VAL. How do I give them a thrill?

MYRA. Don't ask *me* how. You don't have to manipulate their knees to get shoes on them.

VAL. Manipulate their… I never *touch* their knees!

MYRA. I've got eyes in my head!

HUCKSTER. *(Chanting out in the street.)* Ahhhh ahhhh. Turnip greens, new potatoes, rutabagas. Ahhh-ahhh. Carrots, string beans, onions!

MYRA. Also your attitude is very suggestive.

VAL. Suggestive of what, Mrs. Torrance?

MYRA. Bedrooms, if you want to know.

VAL. Bedrooms!

MYRA. Yes!

VAL. That sure is peculiar. How do I do *that*?

MYRA. Everything that you do. The way you talk, the way you walk, every single motion of you. Slew-footing this way and that way like one of those awful, disgustin', carnival dancers!

> *The huckster is heard calling further away. Val stares at Myra with a long, troubled look.*

Quit looking at me like that!

> *She sobs.*

I know how awful I look.

VAL. *(Gently.)* You don't look awful, Myra.

MYRA. Yes, I do—my hair all stringing down—my face always turns so red when I get worked up.

> *She sobs and turns away.*

VAL. *(Very gently.)* Myra—I mean, Mrs. Torrance. I wanted to keep this job. I was tired of moving around and being lonesome and only meeting with strangers. I wanted to feel like I belonged somewhere and lived liked regular people. Instead of like a fox that's chased by hounds!

MYRA. Maybe I haven't understood you exactly.

VAL. No. You haven't.

MYRA. How could I though? You're still a stranger to me. *(Still sobbing a little.)* Well, I don't feel much better acquainted with *you.* Give me one of them tissue paper things.

> *She blows her nose.*

VAL. How do you get to know people? I used to think you did it by touching them with your hands. But later I found out that only made you more of a stranger than ever. Now I know that *nobody* ever gets to *know* anybody.

MYRA. Nobody ever gets to *know* anybody?

VAL. No. Don't you see how it is? We're all of us locked up tight inside our own bodies. Sentenced—you might say—to solitary confinement inside our own skins.

MYRA. *(Giving him a long, puzzled look.)* Is that something out of The Book?

VAL. *(Grinning.)* No. That goes into The Book. I'm going to show you some tricks that I learned from a lady osteopath that took me in.

MYRA. What tricks?

VAL. Do you trust me or don't you?

MYRA. Yeah. I trust you completely, but…

VAL. Well then, lean forward a little and drop your head.

MYRA. You're a queer one. I can't figure out what you *belong* to, exactly.

VAL. Me? Belong to? Nothing.

MYRA. Don't you have folks anywhere?

VAL. I lost track of 'em after they lost their land.

MYRA. They worked on shares?

VAL. No, not shares—but leavings, scraps, tidbits!

MYRA. Where did they go?

VAL. I don't know where. They were loose chicken feathers blown around by the wind.

MYRA. You didn't go with 'em?

VAL. No. No, I made up my mind about something and I've stuck to it ever since.

MYRA. What's that?

VAL. To live by myself. So when the others left, I stayed on Witches Bayou. It was a good place to hide in. Big cypress trees all covered with long gray moss the sun couldn't hardly shine through.

MYRA. Misty-like.

VAL. Yeah.

MYRA. How old were you? How did you live?

VAL. Fourteen. I lived like a fox. I hunted and fished but most of the time I was hungry. I guess it must've made me a little light-headed, because I know I had some peculiar notions… I used to lay out naked in a flatboat with the sun on me.

MYRA. What did you do that for?

VAL. I had a feeling that something *important* was going to come *in* to me.

MYRA. In? Through your skin?

VAL. Kind of. Most people don't expect nothing important to come *in* to them. They just expect to get up early—plow—rest—go turtle-eggin' an' then back to bed. They never look up at the sky, dark—or with stars—or blazing yellow with sunlight—and ask it, "Why? why? why?"

MYRA. Did you ask it, "Why?"

VAL. That was the first word I learned to spell out at school. And I expected some answer. It would come *in* to me. Through my eyes—see? Through my ears, through my skin. Like a net—see? If you don't spread it out, you won't catch nothing in it. But if you do, you *might*. Mine I used to spread it out, wide-open, those afternoons on the bayous—ears pricked, eyes peeled—watchin', waitin', listenin' for it to come!

MYRA. Did it ever?

VAL. No. Never quite. It would of though, if I hadn't gotten thrown off the track by the girl.

MYRA. There was a girl. What girl?

VAL. A girl I met on the bayou.

MYRA. Oh, what about her?

VAL. She was the first one, yeah. That day I was real excited. I had a feeling that if I just kept polin' on a little bit further I'd come bang on whatever it was I was after!

MYRA. And she was it?

VAL. Naw, she *wasn't*. But she made me *think* she was.

MYRA. How did she do that?

VAL. How? By standin' naked on the dogtrot, in the door of the cabin, without a stitch on.

MYRA. What was she like?

VAL. J'ya ever notice the inside of a shell? How white that is?

MYRA. She was young I suppose. Very young?

VAL. Her shape up here, it wasn't no bigger than this *(Slightly cupping his palm.)* I hadn't noticed before the special diff'rence in women.

MYRA. But you did then?

VAL. Yes, I did then.

MYRA. Was she…?

VAL. What?

MYRA. More attractive than—anyone since?

VAL. She was—th' first.

MYRA. What did you do? What happened?

VAL. I poled th' boat up closer. An' she came out on the dogtrot an' stood there awhile with the daylight burnin' around her as bright as heaven as far as I could see! Oh, God, I remember a bird flown out of the moss and its wings made a shadow on her! *(Bows his head.)* An' then it sang a single high clear note. An' as though she was waitin' for that as a kind of a signal—to *trap* me—she turned and smiled an' walked on back in the cabin!

MYRA. And you followed, of course? What was it like inside?

VAL. Inside it was—empty inside.

MYRA. It couldn't have been!

VAL. Well, maybe it wasn't, but all I remember's the bed.

MYRA. Only the bed?

VAL. Made out of cypress an' covered with heaps of moss.

MYRA. Doesn't sound nice.

VAL. Well, it was. She'd been lonesome.

MYRA. How did you know? Did she tell you?

VAL. She didn't have to. She had it carved in her body.

MYRA. Carved? Is lonesomeness carved in people's bodies?

    She unconsciously touches her own.

VAL. Kind of. Anyhow you can see it. Or feel it.

MYRA. *(Softly.)* What did she say to you?

VAL. She couldn't talk much except in some Cajun language. I taught her some words.

MYRA. Such as what?

VAL. Such as *love.*

MYRA. You taught her that?

VAL. It was then I thought I discovered what it was that I'd been hankerin' after all.

MYRA. You thought it was that? You mean she answered "me"?

VAL. Her! Me! Us together! Then afterwards—afterwards I thought that wasn't it. When I'd left her, the satisfaction would leave me an' I'd be…like this. *(Clenches his fist.)* Right on the edge of something tremendous. It wasn't her. She was just a woman, not even a woman quite, and what I wanted was…

MYRA. Was *what*?

VAL. Christ, I don't know. I gotta find out!

MYRA. What did you do after that?

VAL. I settled down for a spell in Texas. Seemed like the restlessness had worn off and I might get connected with something. But things went wrong. Something happened.

MYRA. What?

VAL. Never mind what. But everything was different after that. I wasn't free anymore. I was followed by something I couldn't get off my mind. Till I came here…

MYRA. Well, now that you've come here and got a good job, you can live a regular life and forget all of that.

VAL. I don't forget as easy as you, Mrs. Torrance. You don't even remember that I've lost my job.

MYRA. You haven't lost your job.

VAL. I'm not fired, huh?

MYRA. *(Smiling and shaking her head.)* We both got a little upset but that's over.

VAL. God, I…

MYRA. God you and lady me? *(Laughs.)* What is this place, a funeral parlor? Let's have some lights, some music. Put something on the jukebox.

VAL. What would you like?

MYRA. I like that number with the steel guitars.

VAL. Yeah, that one!

> *He crosses to the confectionery and starts the music; then he comes back.*

Myra, you know the earth turns.

MYRA. Yes.

VAL. It's turning that way. East. And if a man turned west, no matter how fast, he'd still be going the other way, really, because the earth turns so much faster. It's no use to struggle, to try to move against it. You go the way the earth pulls you whether you want to or not. I don't want to touch you, Myra.

MYRA. No, I don't want you to.

VAL. It wouldn't be right for me to.

MYRA. *(Half questioning.)* On account of Jabe?

VAL. No, on account of you. I don't want nothing to hurt you. Let's shake hands.

MYRA. That's not necessary!

> *Without knowing why, she is suddenly angry. She crosses to the foot of the stairs. He follows her to the stairs.*

VAL. You're not still afraid of me, are you?

> *Myra starts quickly upstairs.*

Mrs. Torrance! Myra!

> *Myra pauses a moment on the landing, looking down at him with nervous hesitation. In an intense whisper:*

Myra!

> *She disappears through the door and slams it shut. Val stares in bewilderment.*

SLOW CURTAIN

Scene 2

It is several hours later on the same day. The mellow afternoon sunlight is muted. Val stands in the confectionery archway with his back to the audience. He is staring intently up at a large Coca-Cola ad through the arch. In conjunction with the beverage, this ad forcefully expounds the charms of a "Petty Girl" in a one-piece lemon-yellow bathing suit. She and Val appear to be experiencing a long and silent spiritual communion. In his hand Val has a Coke. Slowly, dreamily, he elevates the bottle to his mouth. Outside, at some distance, a rooster crows longingly at the sun. A man enters the front door in boots and riding breeches, bearing a shotgun. He coughs twice to divert Val's attention from the seductive picture.

VAL. *(Turning.)* Sorry, I was dreaming. Beautiful afternoon, huh?

MAN. I'd like to see Mrs. Torrance.

VAL. She's gone upstairs with her husband. He's not so well.

MAN. Tell her that David Anderson is here.

VAL. Just press that buzzer on the counter and she'll be down.

DAVID. Thank you.

> *Hesitantly he follows this suggestion. The buzzer is heard above. After a moment, the door on the landing opens and Myra appears. She descends a few steps. Then seeing Anderson, she stops short.*

MYRA. *(Sharply, involuntarily.)* David!

> *They exchange a long, wordless stare. Then Myra recovers herself and comes down.*

(To Val.) Will you go to the drugstore for me?

VAL. What do you want?

MYRA. Nothing. I mean some ice cream.

VAL. A pint of vanilla?

> *Myra says nothing. Val looks curiously at them both and goes out.*

MYRA. Well.

DAVID. How are you, Myra?

MYRA. Very well, thanks. How are you?

DAVID. *(Staring at her.)* All right.

> *There is an awkward pause.*

MYRA. You came in here once before and I ordered you out.

DAVID. That was six years ago.

MYRA. No. Eight.

DAVID. Right after your marriage.

MYRA. Not so long after yours.

DAVID. You can't hold a grudge that long.

MYRA. Oh yes I can. I think I can hold one forever. What do you want?

DAVID. Cartridges.

MYRA. You're going out shooting wild birds? I don't have to wish you luck. I haven't forgotten what a good marksman you were. Here's your cartridges. Is there anything else?

DAVID. It seems odd to see you in here, like this.

MYRA. Waiting on trade? Does that seem *common* to you?

DAVID. No. You never were practical, though. You were always such a…

MYRA. *Fool? Yes!* But I've changed since then.

DAVID. You haven't changed in appearance.

MYRA. Some women are like green things. They're kept on ice. I guess I'm one of that kind. You've changed a good deal. I wouldn't have known you at all except for your walk. You still move around like you were the Lord of creation. I should think you might have found out by this time that your ten thousand acres don't make up the whole universe. Other people have got some property, too. I have this store, for instance. I don't have to *clerk* in it either. I *have* a clerk. *(Voice trembles.)* I haven't come down so terribly far in the world.

DAVID. *(Embarrassed.)* Of course you haven't.

MYRA. No, I've gone *up*. And I'm going to go up still *higher*.

DAVID. I'm glad of that, Myra. People have told me about your husband's sickness. I…

MYRA. *(Feverishly.)* Yes. He's dying. After his death I'm planning to sell the store. Sixty or sixty-five thousand it ought to be worth. I'm planning to leave Two River and travel around. Florida, California, New York. I've been an object for pity for a little too long around here. "Poor Myra, she's hopeless, she's crushed!" That isn't exactly the truth and I'm tired of having it whispered behind my back. My life isn't over, my life is only *commencing.* Six ten for the cartridges, please.

DAVID. *(Extending the money.)* Here, Myra.

MYRA. Just put it down on the counter. Now get out. Don't ever come back here again.

DAVID. *(Quietly.)* All right, Myra.

> *He goes slowly out. Myra looks after him. A rooster crows mournfully in the distance. Myra raises her hand to her lips. She looks stunned. Val enters. He grins at her.*

VAL. Finished your talk?

MYRA. *(Vaguely.)* Yes, David.

VAL. David?

MYRA. *(Starting.)* Excuse me, I mean "Val." *(Bitterly.)* I made a fool of myself.

> *The rooster crows.*

VAL. Huh?

MYRA. *(Evasively.)* That rooster always crows about sundown. Sounds like he's remembering something.

> *Jabe knocks on the ceiling.*

I wonder if he *is.*

> *She goes back upstairs. Val opens the ice cream, dips it out with his fingers. Vee Talbott enters, stops short in the doorway as though dazed.*

VAL. Oh, hello, Mrs. Talbott.

VEE. Something's gone wrong with my eyes. I can't see nothing.

VAL. Here, let me help you. You probably drove up here with that setting sun in your face.

VEE. What? Yes. That must be it.

VAL. There now. Sit down right here.

VEE. Oh, thank you so much.

VAL. I haven't seen you since that night you let me sleep in the lockup.

VEE. Has the minister called on you yet? Reverend Tooker? I made him promise he would. I told him that you were new in the community and that you weren't affiliated with any church yet. I want you to visit ours.

VAL. Well, that's mighty gracious of you, Mrs. Talbott.

VEE. The Church of the Resurrection! Episcopal, you know. Some people, especially Catholics, think our church was founded by Henry the Eighth, that horrible, lecherous old man who had as many wives as a cat has lives! There's not a word of truth in it. We have direct Apostolic Succession through St. Paul, who converted the early Angles. Angles is what they called the original English.

VAL. Angles, huh?

VEE. Yes, Angles. Our church is sometimes known as the Anglican Church.

VAL. Well, now, that's right int'restin', Mrs. Talbott. What's that picture you got? Something to put on display?

VEE. I thought that Myra might put it up with the Easter decorations.

VAL. I tell you what. We'll put it on display in the confectionery. Myra is going to do it over for spring. What's this picture of?

VEE. The Church of the Resurrection!

VAL. I didn't recognize it.

VEE. Well, I give it a sort of imaginative treatment.

VAL. Aw. What's this?

VEE. The steeple.

VAL. Is the church steeple red?

VEE. Naw.

VAL. Why did you paint it red then?

VEE. I felt it that way. I always paint a thing the way that it strikes me instead of always the way that it actually is. Appearances are misleading. Nothing is what it looks like to the eyes. You've got to have vision to see. That's why the New Awleuns artists took an in'rest in my work. They say that it shows a lot of vision. Primitive is what they call it and one of my pictures they've hung on exhibition in the Audubon Park Museum! Oh I tell you since I got into this painting, my whole outlook is different. I can't explain how it is, the difference to me.

VAL. You don't have to explain, I know what you mean. Before you started to paint, it didn't make sense.

VEE. What? What didn't?

VAL. Existence.

VEE. No, no it didn't. Existence didn't make sense.

VAL. You need some new shoes.

VEE. Do I?

VAL. Yes, I'll sell you a pair of beautiful wine-colored slippers.

VEE. I don't know.

VAL. Come on. Sit down there. Give me your foot. You got a bad circulation.

VEE. What?

VAL. Your feet are cold. Know why? These here elastic garters are too tight on you. Why don't you leave them off and wear pantyhose, like the other girls do?

VEE. Uh?

VAL. Skittish?

VEE. It's late. I got to be going!

VAL. With one shoe off and one shoe on? "Hey diddle, diddle, my son Tom!" Here, I'll put it back on for you. Just lean on my shoulder a minute.

VEE. No I…

VAL. Watch out. There now! Got your balance?

VEE. Oh, I got to be going!

VAL. *(Puts picture over counter.)* How's that Mrs. Talbott? Okay?

> Vee, still too startled to speak, turns vaguely and barges out

of the door. Val looks after her, then suddenly breaks into lighthearted laughter. Myra comes back downstairs slowly with a tense, concentrated expression. Val smiles.

Myra, did you ever see a red church steeple?

MYRA. *(Absently.)* No.

VAL. *(Chuckling.)* Neither did I.

MYRA. Jabe's took a turn for the worse. I had to give him morphine.

VAL. So?

MYRA. He must be out of his mind; he says such awful things to me. Accuses me of wanting him to die.

VAL. Don't you?

MYRA. No! Death's terrible, Val. You're alive and everything's open and free, and you can go this way or that way, whichever direction you choose. And then all at once the doors start closing on you, the walls creep in, till finally there's just one way you can go—the dark way. Everything else is shut off.

VAL. Yes… *(Then, abruptly.)* You got the sun at the back of your head. It brings the gold out in your hair!

MYRA. *(Diverted.)* Does it?

VAL. Yes, it looks pretty, Myra.

MYRA. It's closing time.

VAL. Uh-huh. I'll put these back on the shelves.

> *He picks up the wedding slippers.*

She had a small foot.

MYRA. Rosemary Wildberger?

VAL. Naw, naw, that Whiteside bitch.

MYRA. I could wear these slippers.

VAL. They'd be too small.

MYRA. You want to bet? Try them on me.

VAL. *(Laughing.)* Okay!

> *He slips the shoes on her feet.*

Pinch, don't they?

MYRA. No, they feel marvelous on me!

VAL. *(Doubting.)* Aw!

MYRA. They do!

> *She looks down at them.*

Silver and white. Why isn't everything made out of silver and white?

VAL. Wouldn't be practical, Myra.

MYRA. Practical? What's that? I never heard of practical before. I wasn't cut out for the mercantile business, Val.

VAL. What was you cut out for?

> *Loon stops outside the door and begins to play his guitar in the fading warmth of the afternoon sun. At first the music is uncertain and sad; then it lifts suddenly into a gay waltz.*

MYRA. *(Enrapt with the music.)* Me cut out for? Silver and white! Music! Dancing! The orchard across from Moon Lake! You don't believe me, do you? Well, look at this. You know where I am? I'm on the Peabody Roof! I'm dancing to music! My dress is made out of *mousseline de soie*! Yes, with silver stars on it! And in my hair I've got lovely Cape jasmine blossoms! I'm whirling; I'm dancing faster and faster! Photographers taking my pictures for the *Commercial Appeal* and for the *Times-Picayune*. I'm surrounded by people. Autograph seekers, they want me to sign my name! But I keep on laughing and dancing and scattering stars and lovely Cape jasmine blossoms!

> *Her rhapsodic speech is suddenly interrupted by Jabe's furious knocking on the ceiling. Her elation is instantly crushed out. She stops dancing.*

I thought he had enough to go to sleep…

VAL. Why don't you give him enough to…?

MYRA. Val! I'm a decent woman.

VAL. What's decent? It's disgusting. Decent is something that's scared like a little white ribbit. I'll give you a better word, Myra.

MYRA. What word is that?

> *The guitar changes back to its original slow melody.*

VAL. Love, Myra. The one I taught the little girl on the bayou.

MYRA. That's an old one.

VAL. You've never heard it before.

MYRA. You're wrong about that, my dear. I heard it mentioned quite often the spring before I got married.

VAL. Jabe?

MYRA. No! By a boy named David.

VAL. Oh. David.

MYRA. We used to go every night to the orchard across from Moon Lake. He used to say, "Love! Love! Love!" And so did I, and both of us meant it, I thought. But he quit me that summer for some aristocratic girl, a girl like Cassandra Whiteside! Of course, after that, what I really wanted was death. But Jabe was the next best thing. Although there wasn't much talk about love between us.

VAL. No. There was nothing but hate. Like the cancer, you wish you could kill him.

MYRA. Don't! You scare me. Don't talk that way.

> *She crosses slowly to the door and Loon sings as the scene dims out.*

Scene 3

> *Immediately following, without a break in the music. Loon stops playing, retreats inside the store, and Sheriff Talbott follows.*

TALBOTT. Hey, Loon! Didn't I see you on Front Street this mawnin' an' tell you to clear out of town?

LOON. *(Entering store.)* I thought you was jokin', Cap'n.

TALBOTT. Well, you made a big mistake. We don't allow no unemployed white transients in this town an' I'll be dogged if I'm gonna put up with colored ones.

LOON. I ain't transient, Cap'n.

TALBOTT. Where you livin'?

LOON. Nowhere, right this minute. Slep' on the levee las' night.

TALBOTT. Where you workin'?

LOON. Nowhere, Cap'n. I'se dispossessed.

TALBOTT. Aw, you'se dispossessed! Where'd you pick up all that fancy langwidge? You mean that Mr. Henley got fed up with your no-'countness an' turned you offen his property?

LOON. He turned me off but not fo' no-'countness. I wuked *hard*.

TALBOTT. If you work hard, you oughta make the state a good road-hand. Come on, you're under arrest.

LOON. What fo', Cap'n.

TALBOTT. Vagrancy. Ten-dollar fine or thirty days hard labor.

LOON. Cap'n Talbott, I likes nine-fifty of bein' able to pay that fine.

TALBOTT. Come along.

VAL. Just a minute. I owe this boy ten dollars on his guitar.

TALBOTT. Huh?

VAL. I just bought his musical instrument off him. Here's the money.

> *Loon starts to turn it over to the sheriff.*

Just a minute. Put that in your pocket. You can't fine a man for vagrancy when he's got ten dollars, can you, Sheriff? Not if I'm acquainted with the law.

TALBOTT. Huh?

VAL. He's also got a job. Hey, Loon, you drop back in tonight an' give me a *lesson* on this thing. Okay?

LOON. Yes, suh! Okay!

> *He shuffles hurriedly out. The sheriff stares hard and silently at Val. Val casually strums a chord on the guitar. Deputy Sheriff Pee Wee Bland wobbles ponderously into the doorway laughing heartily, having just delivered some witticism to the men on the porch. He notices the tension and beckons the others to enter. They have all been drinking.*

MYRA. *(Reentering, nervously.)* Val, take these boxes…

TALBOTT. *(Interrupting.)* Just a minute.

> *He catches Val's arm as Val starts to move past him. Val jerks his arm free. All this happens very rapidly.*

You beat the county out of a good road-hand.

VAL. I thought he might be better as a musician.

TALBOTT. Musician, hell! That worthless no'count nigger?

VAL. A man's not worthless because he's dispossessed.

PEE WEE. Hear, hear! *Dispossessed!*

FIRST MAN. Where'd he pick up that Nawthun radical lingo?

SECOND MAN. Who's he talkin' about?

FIRST MAN. That nigger, Loon.

SECOND MAN. Come down here to organize our niggers?

FIRST MAN. Make them bosses, huh? Us chop their cotton for 'em?

PEE WEE. It's talk like that that's back of all our colored tenant trouble.

> *He wobbles up to Val.*

Dispossessed? Did you say *dispossessed*?

VAL. Yes, I *did*.

PEE WEE. How yuh figure a man can be dispossessed from somethin' that never was his'n.

VAL. The land belongs to the man that works the land!

PEE WEE. Hear, hear!

FIRST MAN. That's red talk!

SECOND MAN. Yeah, go back to Rooshuh!

FIRST MAN. Anybody don't like this guvement oughta go back to Rooshuh!

SECOND MAN. Pack 'em all off togethuh, Jews, and radicals, and niggers! Ship 'em all back to *Rooshuh*!

FIRST MAN. Back to Africa with 'em!

MYRA. *(Frightened.)* Sheriff, stop this disturbance! My husband is sick upstairs!

TALBOTT. Quiet down, you boys!

PEE WEE. *(Very drunk and sententious, he talks like a Southern orator of the old school.)* Yeh, you all hush up. I'm talkin' to this young fellow. Now, looky here: a nigger works on a white man's property, don't he? White man houses him an' feeds him an' pays him livin' wages as long as he *produces*. But when he *don't*, it's like my daddy said, he's gotta be blasted out a th' ground like a *daid tree stump* befo' you can run a *plow* th'ough it!

> *A third man enters; he is a huge lout.*

THIRD MAN. What's this here?

FIRST MAN. Some redneck peckerwood with a nawthun edjication's tellin' us how we oughta run our niggers!

MYRA. Sheriff, make them stop right now!

PEE WEE. That nigger, Loon, got dispossessed from nothin'. The land wasn't his.

VAL. No, nothin' was his. Nothin' but his own black skin and that was his damnation!

FIRST MAN. Listen to that!

SECOND MAN. The carpetbaggers are comin' back agin!

THIRD MAN. *(Going up to Val.)* You know what I do when I see a snake?

VAL. No, what?

MYRA. Val!

THIRD MAN. I get me a good fork stick to pin it down with. Then I scotch it under the heel of my boot—I scotch its goddam yellow gizzards out!

SECOND MAN. Go *on*!

FIRST MAN. *Show* him, Pinkie.

MYRA. Sheriff! Please!

> *The Third Man spits at Val's shoe.*

VAL. You spit on my shoe! *Wipe it off!*

> *He spits again. Val knocks him down. The men close in about Val like a pack of hounds. There is a near riot for a few moments. Then the sheriff disperses them.*

TALBOTT. Come on, you all! Clear out! *Clear* out! Pee Wee, you're deputy. Git these men out of here!

> *The men are shoved out, grumbling.*

MYRA. Those drunken stave-mill workers make nothing but trouble—

TALBOTT. *(To Val.)* Who are you? What's your name?

VAL. Val Xavier.

MYRA. Val didn't mean anything; he just a talker.

TALBOTT. Where do you come from?

VAL. Any number of places!

> *He picks up the guitar again.*

MYRA. Down state—Witches Bayou.

TALBOTT. Let him answer for himself, Mizz Torrance.

MYRA. Well, don't snap questions at him like he was up on trial. I know everything about this boy.

TALBOTT. You do, huh?

MYRA. Yes, I do. He come to me with the highest recommendations.

TALBOTT. Who from?

MYRA. Friends, relatives. He likes to talk. He's done some writing, but he's no more radical than you or me! I give you my trusted word on it.

TALBOTT. It ain't a question of doubtin' your word, Mizz Torrance.

MYRA. All right. Goodbye. I'm closin' up the store.

TALBOTT. Just one more question, please. What's your draft number, buddy?

> *Val stares at him and strikes a chord on the guitar.*

What's your draft number?

MYRA. *(Quickly.)* Eight thousand an' something. Val, take those empty shoeboxes out to the incinerator!

> *Val goes out with the boxes.*

TALBOTT. How do you happen to know his draft number?

MYRA. He happened to tell me this mawning. Is there anything else that I can do for you, Sheriff?

TALBOTT. Yes, ma'am. You can do yourself a favor an' get a new clerk. That impudent young peckerwood won't bring yuh nothin' but trouble. G'night.

> *The sheriff goes out. Myra leans exhaustedly against the door. Val reenters slowly.*

MYRA. Oh, Val, Val. Why didn't you hold your tongue?

VAL. A man has got to stick up for his own kind of people.

MYRA. That old colored beggar, Loon?

VAL. We're both of us dispossessed. Just give me my wages an' I'll be moving along.

> *Myra stares at him speechlessly.*

MYRA. Val, I don't want you to go.

VAL. I'd ruin your business for you.

MYRA. Never mind that.

VAL. Besides I'm under suspicion now, and it wouldn't be safe.

MYRA. Just wait. This'll all blow over.

VAL. No. There's something I didn't mention about me this mawning.

MYRA. What happened in Texas?

VAL. Yes. I'm *wanted*, Myra.

MYRA. You're *wanted*?

> *Val gravely picks up the guitar without looking at Myra and strikes a slow chord on it.*

What are you *wanted* for, Val.

VAL. *(Quietly, without looking up.)* For rape.

MYRA. What?

VAL. Rape!

MYRA. Shhh! I don't believe it. That's something *nigguhs* are lynched for—not *you*, Val.

VAL. Yes, me.

> *He strikes a chord on the guitar.*

MYRA. Who was the woman?

> *Val punctuates his speech with strumming on the guitar, which he never puts down till the end of the scene. He avoids Myra's eyes.*

VAL. A woman from Waco, Texas. Wife of an oil-field superintendent. A plain sort of woman; I never noticed her much. One night her husband got drunk. Passed out in the car. This woman from Waco come to my room that night. Afterwards, I was disgusted with her and with me, I said to her, "Listen, I don't want nothing like this; I'm getting away!" "I'm goin' with yuh," she said. "Oh, no you're not," I told her, "I travel alone." She started to scream. She run to the phone and screamed that she'd been raped. I lost my head for a minute and struck her in the mouth. I drove clean out of Texas before daybreak. But not long afterwards, though, I begun to see my name and my description in public buildings—"Wanted for Rape in Texas."

MYRA. You've changed your name.

VAL. Yes, but not my description.

MYRA. That's why you're quitting this job.

VAL. Not just for that reason. I have another reason.

MYRA. What's that?

VAL. *You.* Like I told you this morning, I oughtn't to touch you, but I keep *wanting* to, Myra.

MYRA. Oh.

VAL. You don't get rid of something by holding it in. It gathers, it grows, it gets to be *enormous.*

MYRA. Yes.

VAL. You said this morning I touched the women too much when I tried shoes on them. Maybe I do. My hands—I'm afraid of my hands. I hold them in so hard the muscles ache.

>   *He strikes a chord sharply.*

You know what it's like? A herd of elephants, straining at a rope. How do I know the rope won't break sometime? With you or with somebody else?

MYRA. *(Going slowly to the door. She touches her forehead.)* My head's still whirling from all that excitement in here. I don't seem able to *think.* The cotton gin bothers me, too. It makes a sound like your heart was pounding a lot too fast.

VAL. Mine does sometimes. *(Strumming.)*

MYRA. Everyone's does sometimes.

VAL. Your belt's untied in the back.

MYRA. Is it? Fix it for me.

Slowly Val sets down the guitar on the counter; crossing slowly to her, he touches her waist.

VAL. You come way in at the middle.

MYRA. I haven't let go of my figure like some women do. I don't feel everything's done for me yet. I lived in a state of—what do they call it?—artificial respiration. Something that pumps the breath in and out of your body when otherwise you'd be dead. Dead as a rock is, Val! *(Turns abruptly to him.)* Oh, Val, I don't want you to go. I'll make it all right. I'll fix things up so nobody's going to suspicion. I'll make up all kinds of stories if you'll stay here! Huh? Huh, Val?

VAL. *(Hoarsely.)* Myra…

MYRA. Yes?

VAL. Let's—let's—go in the back room a minute.

> *The cotton gin can be heard in the distance.*

MYRA. That room's locked, Val.

VAL. Where's the key?

MYRA. I took it an' thrown it away.

VAL. What did you do that for?

MYRA. Because I known you would ask me to go in there sometime an' I was scared I might do it.

> *He releases her and goes quickly out through the confectionery. The gin seems to pump even louder. After a moment Val returns to the room.*

VAL. *(In a hoarse whisper.)* That lock was no good, Myra.

MYRA. You broke it open?

VAL. Yes.

MYRA. Christ! I was scared that you would.

> *For a long moment they stare at each other, then rush together in a convulsive embrace.*

CURTAIN

ACT THREE

SCENE: *The same, but the room in the rear through the arch has been redecorated. The walls have been painted pale blue and have been copiously hung with imitation dogwood blossoms to achieve a striking effect of an orchard in full bloom. The room is almost subjective, a mood or a haunting memory beyond the drab actuality of the dry-goods department. Its lighting fixtures have been covered with Japanese lanterns so that, when lighted, they give the room a soft, rosy glow. It is a rainy spring afternoon about two months after the preceding scene. The old-fashioned lights of the store cannot entirely dispel the silvery gloom. The Gothic features of the room are accentuated by this shadowy effect. Val is alone in the store. He is working on his book, the loose pages of which he keeps in a battered old tin box. He writes with a stub pencil which he chews reflectively, then scribbles with rapt expression. The jukebox is playing a number. He looks very simple and lonely, a little faunlike, seated on one of the low shoe-fitting stools, absorbed in his creative labor. There is a faint whisper of rain, and of wind. Myra enters from the street in a transparent white raincoat, very glowing and warm and happy. Val quickly stuffs the script back in the box and pushes it out of sight.*

MYRA. Hello, hello, hello! What are you hiding from me? Is it the book? Ah, the mysterious book. I never was quite sure that it existed.

VAL. What d'ja think it was?

MYRA. Something you dreamed those afternoons on the bayou! Let me look at it.

VAL. No.

MYRA. Let me just hold it.

VAL. Don't be silly.

MYRA. Please!

He surrenders the bundle of papers grudgingly.

Such a big book, too; so good an' solid.

VAL. It's got life in it, Myra. When people read it, they're going to be frightened. They'll say it's crazy because it tells the truth! Now, give it back to me, Myra. It's not finished yet.

MYRA. I wish that I had something to do with it, too.

She laughs tenderly, and hands it back to him.

I had a wonderful time this afternoon. After I got Jabe's new prescription, I drove over to Tupelo to get my hair done. I knew it would be my last chance before Easter. How does it look, Val?

VAL. Great.

MYRA. How're things going?

VAL. Slow. I haven't rung up a single cash-sale since noon.

MYRA. Rain, rain. You certainly kill our trade. I was stuck on th' road coming home for nearly an hour before I got pulled out.

She takes off her raincape and puts on a bright smock.

I kind of enjoyed it, though. The air was so fresh, an' when the bells started ringing…

VAL. What're they ringing for?

MYRA. Good Friday church service. Dr. Hector is preaching the Seven Last Words from the Cross. Just as they started to ring, a big white moth flew in the car window. Val, I hate most bugs, but this one I felt a kind of a sympathy for. He was terribly young.

VAL. How do you know he was young? Did you ask him his age?

MYRA. No, but he had that surprised, inexperienced look about him that young things have. It was easy to see he had just come from the cocoon, and was *sooo* disappointed. Of cou'se he expected th' world t' be bright an' gold, but what he found was a nasty, cold spring rain. His two long whiskers were covered with strings of pearls. He sat on the steering wheel an' shook them off. I asked him, "Why?" An' he said, "Don'tcha know? It's in bad taste to put on pearls before dark!"

VAL. You're talking foolishness, Myra.

MYRA. Am I? Fo'give me, da'ling. I'm in that kind of a humor. My

God, you got eyes that shine in th' dark like a dawg's.

> *She starts humming a tune.*

Remember that? Such—a long time ago. Before Columbus discovered America even. Oh, beautiful fo' spacious skies, for amber fields of grain. …Greta Garbo is at the Delta Brilliant. …Fo' purple mountain majesties, above the fruited… What's these here?

VAL. Women's soft-sole slippers. They just come in.

> *Impulsively she gathers them up like an armful of plushy red flowers and tosses them into the air.*

MYRA. *(Ecstatically.)* Wake me early, Mother, fo' I shall be Queen of the May!

VAL. For Chrissakes, Myra, what did'ja do that for?

MYRA. Oh, soft-sole slippers. Women's soft-sole slippers! They seem t' be so damned unnecessary!

VAL. What's the matter with you this afternoon?

MYRA. When people have dreams, unusually good dreams, they get up singing, they go to the beauty parlor, and act like fools all day! When serious-minded people who write big books say, "What's th' matter with you?" they simply smile an' say, "We have our secrets."

> *Val opens the door.*

The rain's slacked up?

VAL. Yeah, a little.

MYRA. That's good. Maybe we'll have a nice bright Easter, Val. We'll go to church an' look so lovely the Lawd will have to fo'give us for all our sins!

VAL. *(In the doorway.)* River's way up over flood-stage at Friar's Point Landing. They say sometimes this place is cut off by water.

MYRA. They say! They say! What of it? Ten thousand years from today we'll just be little telltale marks on the sides of rocks which people refer to as fossils.

> *There is the sound of slow tolling bells across the wide, rainy fields.*

That's all will be left of our big tremendous adventures!

> *She smiles with amazement at this thought.*

Teeny-weeny little pencil-scratches, things like pigeon tracks will be what's left of Myra—what's left of Val! Then old Mr. Important Scientific Professor will pick up his microscope—"Humph!" he'll say, "This girl had remarkable legs." Or, "Goodness, this young man lost a rib somewhere." That will be all they'll ever find out about us! Were we in love? Were we happy? Did white moths fly in our windows? How do they know? They can't tell. History isn't written about *little* people. All that little people ever get to be is marks on rocks called *fossils.*

VAL. Yes, unless they write books or something.

MYRA. Oh, yes, of course, unless they write books or something! Then they're remembered *always*!

> *She jumps down from the ladder and hugs him tenderly against her.*

You will be, da'ling! Don't worry!

VAL. Sarcasm?

MYRA. No, not a bit!

> *She laughs gently.*

You're such a wonderful, wonderful baby! When I'm a fossil, even if it makes Mr. Science Professor blush, I hope he discovers my scratches are all scrambled up with yours.

> *She laughs gaily. A small Negro boy enters the store.*

Wipe yo' feet off, Bennie, don't track the floor.

BENNIE. Yes, ma'am.

MYRA. What do you want? Peanuts?

BENNIE. I wan' peanuts, but granny wan' a nickel's worth a snuff.

MYRA. Aw. Well, Granny's got to have her snuff, now, don't she? How is Granny feelin'?

BENNIE. She been laid up in bed with breakbone fever.

MYRA. Aw, now, that's a shame. You tell 'er Mizz Torrance say to get well quick, quick, quick, 'cause we can't do without 'er.

> *Loon enters in overalls.*

BENNIE. Yes, ma'am.

LOON. Howdy, Mizz Torr'nce.

MYRA. Hello, Loon. Val, give Bennie a bag full a goobers, will yuh? They're on th' house.

LOON. *(Admiringly.)* You sho' are gracious, ma'am. I wunder if you would take my note for somethin'?

MYRA. Loon, I've got enough notes from you to paper th' store with already. What do you want?

LOON. A little plug tobacco.

MYRA. Well, put your cross on this.

BENNIE. Thank you.

LOON. Thanks, ma'am.

> *Bennie comes back out with the peanuts and goes out the front door. There is a sound of shouting.*

MYRA. Oh, they're shouting up over there at the big Lent meeting. Sounds like they might be hitting the sawdust trail.

LOON. Will be before sundown.

MYRA. How 'bout you, Loon?

LOON. Me hit it? Now, I guess I glories too much in the flesh for that. Good afternoon, Mizz Torrance.

MYRA. *(To Loon.)* Good afternoon. Where you takin' that load of sandbags to?

LOON. Down river t' Mr. Sikeses.

MYRA. You think there's a chance the levee might go out?

LOON. Ah reckon not unless th' Lawd intends it to. G'by, ma'am.

MYRA. Goodbye.

> *Loon starts the mules. His wagon wheels are heard.*

Val?

> *There is no answer. She switches on the lights in the confectionery. Spring blooms with a soft radiance for an instant and then dies out as she releases the switch.*

Val?

> *She turns smiling slightly, her lips moving as she whispers, excitedly, to herself. With a sudden, rapturous awareness she*

draws her hands up the front of her body and clasps them over her breasts.

Oh…

In the archway there is suspended a string of Chinese glass pendants with a tiny gong. With an impulse of childish gaiety, she sets the pendants tinkling, softly, musically, in the store's greenish gloom and she laughs to herself with a child's quick, delicate laughter. While her back is turned, the Conjure Man glides noiselessly into the store. Now, for the first time, there is a low muttering of thunder. The lights in the confectionery flicker a little. Still unaware of the Conjure Man's presence, Myra shivers slightly and a bewildered, uncertain look appears on her face and she raises a hand to touch her cheek and her forehead. As though with a disturbing prescience of something unnatural, she turns about slowly and meets the Negro's gaze. She catches her breath in a sudden, sharp gasp. The Conjure Man smiles and makes a slight obeisance. He stretches out his small clawlike hand, in the hollow of which he is presenting some object. Myra, breathlessly:

What—what do you want?

The Conjure Man mumbles something which cannot be heard.

What? No! No, I don't want it. (*Then, smiling defiantly.*) I don't need holy stones to bring me luck.

The Conjure Man makes another slight bow, then starts to turn away.

If you want to make an honest dollar, though, you can go out back and wash the Mississippi Delta off my car. You'll find a sponge, a bucket, and a bunch of old chamois hanging in the garage.

The Conjure Man mumbles some eager words of thanks and starts to enter the confectionery. Myra looks after him, troubled, not knowing why. In the archway he stops and looks back over his shoulder to meet her gaze. There is a moment of curiously tense stillness. Then he grins and makes another slight bow and disappears. There is the sound of low thunder again. The front door opens and Dolly comes in.

DOLLY. Has he gone?

MYRA. Who?

DOLLY. The Conjure Man—from Blue Mountain. When I first caught a sight of him out there, I swear to goodness I neahly had a conniption! I was scared to death that he would *mark* my *baby*! Which reminds me to ask you! Have those maternity garments got here yet?

MYRA. No, they haven't come yet.

DOLL. What? I ordered 'em two months ago.

MYRA. I know, and I can't understand what's causin' the delay.

DOLLY. Neither can I. My God, what am I going to do?

MYRA. I'm sorry.

DOLLY. I guess I'll have to hang out a sign, "Excuse me, people."

Myra turns away in distaste. Beulah rushes in.

BEULAH. Excitement! Cassandra Whiteside's come in town drunk as a lord.

DOLLY. No.

BEULAH. I just seen her on Front Street. Wearin' a white satin evenin' dress. She's been in another wreck; the side of the car's bashed in.

DOLLY. I thought they revoked her license.

BEULAH. She's got her a nigger chauffeur. At least I *hope* he's a chauffeur.

DOLLY. Beulah.

BEULAH. Well, there has been a great deal of speculation about 'em that's not very pleasant. They say that she's been ostracized in Memphis, asked to leave sev'ral parties; and her father has actually received a warning note from the Klan.

DOLLY. Goodness. She'll be worse than ostracized if she keeps up at this rate.

BEULAH. Myra, what will you do if she comes in here and starts to make a disturbance?

MYRA. *(Shortly.)* Put her out.

BEULAH. You think you could? They say she fights like a tiger.

MYRA. *(As Val enters.)* I think Val would be able to handle her for me.

VAL. *(Setting the boxes down.)* What did you call me for, Myra?

MYRA. *(Confused.)* Call you? Oh, yes, I—I can't remember just now.

BEULAH. That sounds extremely suspicious. *(Winks.)*

DOLLY. Don't it, though? Look, they're blushing.

BEULAH. Both of them. Oh, I think it's marvelous to see a man who can blush.

MYRA. *(With nervous haste.)* Val, are those the new Keds?

VAL. No, women's rubbers.

MYRA. Just in time for the rain; how very lucky.

DOLLY. *(Meaningfully.)* How's Jabe?

MYRA. *(Still confused.)* Jabe?

DOLLY. Yes, your husband, honey. Jabe Torrance.

MYRA. Jabe's no better.

DOLLY. Ain't that turr'ble!

BEULAH. I don't guess you *could* look for much improvement.

MYRA. No. All we can do is try to relieve the pain. Val, bring up the rest of those boxes and stack them up there.

>*Val is glad to get out.*

DOLLY. Myra, that green is your color!

BEULAH. Don't it look sweet on her, though? I had my eye on that dress; it's the nices' thing you had in stock, Myra Torrance.

MYRA. It's more of a blue than a green.

BEULAH. What do they call it?

MYRA. *(With a slight, suppressed smile.)* They call it "ecstasy blue."

DOLLY. I swan.

>*She exchanges a significant look with Beulah.*

BEULAH. But don't it become her, though? It brings the gold out in her hair.

DOLLY. *It does.*

MYRA. I just had it washed. That always brightens the color.

DOLLY. What with? Goldenfoam?

MYRA. No, with a few drops of lemon. That's all I use.

DOLLY. Honestly? Well, she's took on more *sparkle* this spring.

BEULAH. I think it's wonderful that you can be so brave.

MYRA. What do you mean?

BEULAH. Why, I mean about Jabe's condition.

MYRA. Oh, excuse me a minute. I gotta take Jabe his medicine. He's been so restless today.

> *She goes back upstairs. Beulah looks at Dolly and giggles. Dolly looks at Beulah and giggles an octave higher. They both cover their mouths as the Temple Sisters enter.*

BLANCH. I want you to know…

EVA. Dr. Hector had just finished preaching the Seven Last Words from the Cross…

BLANCH. When who should we run into…

EVA. Yes! on Front Street.

BEULAH. Sandra Whiteside?

EVA and BLANCH. Yes!

DOLLY. I know. We just been talking.

EVA. She is blowing her car horn at the Red Crown Station.

BLANCH. They gave the service attendant instructions not to service her car.

EVA. And she is blowing, and blowing and blowing on her horn drawing a big crowd there.

BLANCH. I thought her parents agreed to keep her out of Two River County for good.

EVA. What's that she was shouting Blanch?

BLANCH. *(Eva repeating.)* Behold Cassandra! Shouting doom at the gates.

EVA. And some bright-skin nigger was in the car with her. It's really created a perfectly terrible stir.

BLANCH. Imagine—on Good Friday!

EVA. Utterly shameless! Where's that nice-looking young man?

BLANCH. I got to return those shoes. I went to a very expensive podiatrist in Memphis. He said they'd ruined my feet. Why Palm Sunday mawning I couldn't hardly march in church with the choir. Mr. Xavier. Oh, they've opened the confectionery. She had it redecorated.

EVA. Oh, look at the confectionery. All done over. She says it's supposed to resemble the orchard across from Moon Lake.

MYRA. *(Upstairs.)* Jabe.

BEULAH. What's that?

DOLLY. Can you make it out?

MYRA. Jabe!

BEULAH. *(Going to the foot of the steps.)* What's that shouting upstairs?

JABE. No, I won't take it.

MYRA. The doctor prescribed it for you. It helps the pain.

JABE. I know what you're trying to do. You're trying to kill me.

DOLLY. What?

BEULAH. What?

MYRA. You're out of your head.

DOLLY. What's that?

BLANCH. Sssh.

EVA. Sssh.

MYRA. Jabe, you don't know what you're saying.

> *The door bangs open.*

I'll call for the doctor.

BLANCH. Delirious!

EVA. Yes, out of his haid!

MYRA. Val! Val!

DOLLY. I'll get him for yuh, Myra! Mr. Xavier.

> *There is great excitement. Val comes in.*

VAL. What's the matter?

BLANCH. Oh, something's goin' on, I don't know what…

EVA. But it's awful!

Myra appears above.

MYRA. *Val?*

VAL. Yeah?

MYRA. Phone Dr. Bob, and tell him to come right over!

She slams the door.

EVA. Where's Dr. Bob?

BLANCH. Ain't he in Jackson Springs?

EVA. I'm very much afraid the wires are down!

VAL. *(Lifting the phone.)* Get me Jackson Springs. *(Into the phone.)* Jackson Springs? The wires are down.

MYRA. I've got to get in touch with Dr. Bob!

Her hair is disarranged, and her dress torn open as though she had been in a struggle.

Jabe's delirious. He wouldn't take the morphine. Did you hear him? He said I was trying to kill him!

She picks up the receiver, jiggles it.

EVA. Val tried to phone.

BLANCH. They told him the wires were down.

MYRA. Then I'll just have to drive over.

BLANCH. Oh, but they say there's danger of the bridge collapsing.

MYRA. What else can I do?

EVA. Blanch, if you were married and your husband was desperately ill, wouldn't you take a chance on the bridge collapsing?

BLANCH. No, I certainly wouldn't. No, I certainly… Oh, before you go, Myra—about these shoes…

MYRA. *(Snatching a raincoat from the closet.)* Oh, I'm distracted, I—Val, tell the nigger to put the chains on the tires!

VAL. I can't do six things at once. Miss Eva here wants some money back on a pair of shoes.

MYRA. Money back? What money? You got the shoes for nothing!

BLANCH. Oh, horrors, don't you remember how I tripped over that rubber mat an' practickly broke my ankle?

EVA. Two trips to the doctor it cost us!

BLANCH. Ten dollars!

EVA. But we'll take eight since Myra has been so…

MYRA. Thanks. Val, give the ladies eight dollars out of the cashbox. Now if you'll excuse me…

BEULAH. Myra, if there's anything I can do.

DOLLY. Don't hesitate to call on me if they is.

> *Myra has already disappeared through the confectionery.*

BLANCH. Gracious…

EVA. Sakes alive! What excitement! Blanch, you go up an' sit with Cousin Jabe.

BLANCH. Oh, I couldn't. I'm having palpitations!

VAL. You all better go or you'll get bogged down on th' road.

DOLLY. Come on, Beulah, let's go! Blanch, you an' Eva comin'?

BLANCH. Just a minute! What happened to those old shoes? You see 'em, Mr. Xavier?

VAL. I thrown 'em in the trash bin. You want 'em back?

BLANCH. Please.

EVA. We couldn't wear 'em, of course, but it's no use throwin' 'em away.

BLANCH. No. Willful waste makes woeful want, they say.

> *She giggles as they back skittishly out of the door.*

Don't you feel it? The atmosphere is simply *charged* with electric disturbance!

> *Val is left alone. He picks up the canvas. Vee Talbott appears through the window as if blind and demented, stiff, groping gestures, shielding her eyes with one arm as she feels along the store window for the entrance, gasping for breath. Val steps aside, taking hold of her arm to guide her into the store. For a few moments she leans weakly, blindly panting for breath against the oval glass of the door, then calls out.*

VEE. I'm—*struck blind!*

VAL. You can't see?

VEE. —No! Nothing…

VAL. *(Assisting her to stool below counter.)* Set down here, Mrs. Talbott.

VEE. —Where?

VAL. *(Pushing her gently.)* Here.

> *Vee sinks moaning onto stool.*

What hurt your eyes, Mrs. Talbott, what happened to your eyes?

VEE. *(Drawing a long, deep breath.)* The vision I waited and prayed for all my life long!

VAL. You had a vision?

VEE. I saw the eyes of my Saviour!—They struck me blind.

> *Leans forward, clasping her eyes in anguish.*

Ohhhh, they burned out my eyes!

VAL. Lean back.

VEE. Eyeballs burn like fire…

VAL. *(Going off R.)* I'll get you something cold to put on your eyes.

VEE. I knew a vision was coming, oh, I had many signs!

VAL. *(In confectionery.)* It must be a terrible shock to have a vision…

> *He speaks gravely, gently, scooping chipped ice from the soft-drink cooler and wrapping it in his handkerchief.*

VEE. *(With the naïveté of a child, as Val comes back to her.)* I thought I would see my Saviour on the day of His Resurrection not of his crucifixion, not Good Friday, Easter that's when I expected to see him but I was mistaken.

> *Val places handkerchief over her eyes.*

—this afternoon, somehow I pulled myself together and walked outdoors and started to go to pray in the empty church and meditate on the Rising of Christ Sunday. Along the road as I walked, thinking about the mysteries of Easter, veils!— *(She makes a long shuddering word out of "veils.")* seemed to drop off my eyes! Light, oh, light! I never have seen such brilliance! It *PRICKED* my eyeballs like *NEEDLES!*

VAL. —Light?

VEE. Yes, yes, light. You know, you know we live in light and shadow, that's, that's what we *live* in, a world of—*light* and—*shadow*…

VAL. Yes. In light and shadow.

> *He nods with complete understanding and agreement. They are like two children who have found life's meaning, simply and quietly, along a country road.*

VEE. A world of light and shadow is what is what we live in, and—it's—confusing…

VAL. Yeah, they—*do* get—*mixed*…

VEE. Well, and then— *(Hesitates to recapture her vision.)* —I heard this clap of thunder! Sky!—Split open!—And there in the split-open sky, I saw, I tell you, I *saw* the TWO HUGE BLAZING EYES OF JESUS CHRIST RISEN!—Not crucified but Risen! I mean Crucified and *then* Risen!—The blazing eyes of Christ Risen! And then a great— *(Raises both arms and makes a great sweeping motion to describe an apocalyptic disturbance of the atmosphere.)* —His hand!—*Invisible!* I didn't *see* his hand!—But it *touched* me—here!

> *She seizes Val's hand and presses it to her great heaving bosom.*

TALBOTT. *(Appearing R. in confectionery, furiously.)* VEE!

> *She starts up, throwing the compress from her eyes. Utters a sharp gasp and staggers backward with terror and blasted ecstasy and dismay and belief, all confused in her look.*

VEE. You!

TALBOTT. VEE!

VEE. *You!*

TALBOTT. *(Advancing.)* VEE!

VEE. *(Making two syllables of the word "eyes.")* —The Ey-es!

> *She collapses forward, falls to her knees, her arms thrown about Val. He seizes her to lift her. Two or three men are peering in at the store window.*

TALBOTT. *(Pushing Val away.)* Let go of her, don't put your hands on my wife!

> *He seizes her roughly and hauls her to the door. Val moves up to help Vee.*

Don't move.

VAL. I'm not goin' nowhere.

TALBOTT. Stand back under that light.

VAL. Which light?

TALBOTT. That light.

> He points; Val goes behind counter.

I want to look at you while I run through some photos of men wanted.

VAL. I'm not wanted.

TALBOTT. A good-looking boy like you is always wanted.

> Men chuckle. Val stands in hot light under green-shaded bulb. Talbott shuffles through photos he has removed from his pocket.

—How tall are you, boy?

VAL. Never measured.

TALBOTT. How much do you weigh?

VAL. Never weighed.

TALBOTT. Got any scars or marks of identification on your face or body?

VAL. No, sir.

TALBOTT. Open your shirt.

VAL. What for?

> He doesn't.

TALBOTT. What did you do before?

VAL. Before—what?

TALBOTT. Before you come here?

VAL. Traveled.

TALBOTT. Awrighty Boy, but I'm gonna tell you something. They's a certain county I know of which has a big sign at the county line that says, "Nigger, don't let the sun go down on you in this county." That's all it says, it don't threaten nothing, it just says, "Nigger, don't let the sun go down on you in this county!"

> Chuckles hoarsely. Rises and takes a step toward Val.

Well, son! You ain't a nigger and this is not that county, but, son, I want you to just imagine that you seen a sign that said to you: "Boy, don't let the sun rise on you in this county." You'll simplify my job by not allowing the sun tomorrow to rise on you in this county. 'S that understood, now, boy?

> *Val stares at him, expressionless, panting.*

(Crossing to door.) I *hope* so. I don't like *violence.*

> *The Conjure Man comes back into the archway, gliding noiselessly as before. He stares inscrutably at Val's back. Val turns, as Myra had turned, with the same air of troubled presentiment, and catches the Conjure Man's gaze. Unconsciously he raises his hands to draw his shirt closer about his throat as though the air had turned colder.*

VAL. What—what do you want?

> *The Conjure Man mumbles almost indistinguishably.*

Oh. Sure. You can stay back there all night, if it don't stop raining!

> *The Conjure Man grins and bows, then extends his palm with the lucky token.*

Huh? Naw, naw, naw, I don't want it! Sorry but I don't truck with that conjure stuff.

> *The Conjure Man bows once more and disappears as noiselessly as he came. There is a low muttering of thunder. Val looks uneasy. He takes off his working jacket. There is a wild burst of drunken laughter outside. The door is thrown open and Sandra enters, a flash of lightning behind her. Her hair hangs loose and she wears a rain-spattered, grass-stained white satin evening gown.*

SANDRA. Behold Cassandra, shouting doom at the gates!

VAL. What do you want?

SANDRA. Oh. It's you. Snakeskin. Remember we're even now.

VAL. What do you want in here?

SANDRA. Protection. I'm in danger.

VAL. Danger of what?

SANDRA. Immolation at the hands of the outraged citizens of Two Rivers County. They've confiscated the nigger that drove my car and ordered me out of Two Rivers.

VAL. You must've given 'em some provocation.

SANDRA. Plenty of provocation. They say that I run around wild and stir up trouble—and neither parental nor civil law is able to restrain me. Why, only this afternoon I was on Cypress Hill with that bright-skinned nigger. They suspect me of having improper relations with him.

VAL. Did you?

SANDRA. No, I poured a libation of wine on my great aunt's grave. But they don't believe me. The Vigilantes decided that I was *persona non grata* and warned me to leave before something bad happened to me. How about you?

VAL. Huh?

SANDRA. Why don't you come along with me? You an' me, we belong to the fugitive kind. We live on motion. Think of it, Val. Nothing but motion, motion, mile after mile, keeping up with the wind, or even faster! Doesn't that make you hungry for what you live on?

> *Val shakes his head.*

Maybe we'll find something new, something never discovered. We'll stake out our claim before the others get to it. What do you say?

> *Val turns away.*

Where's Myra?

VAL. She's gone to Jackson Springs to get a doctor.

SANDRA. Good! We're alone together.

VAL. What's good about it?

SANDRA. Why do you hate me, Val?

VAL. I don't want trouble.

SANDRA. Am I trouble?

VAL. Yeah. As fine a piece of trouble as ever I've seen.

SANDRA. Is Myra trouble?

VAL. Leave her out of it.

SANDRA. Don't you think I know what's going on?

VAL. What are you talking about?

SANDRA. I saw her in Tupelo this morning, having her hair fixed up! What radiance! What joy!

VAL. Shut up about Myra.

SANDRA. Oh, you'd better watch out. It isn't kiss and goodbye with a woman like that! She'll want to keep you forever. I'm not like that.

VAL. Aw, leave me alone.

> *He takes his jacket from a hook.*

SANDRA. I'm not like that!

> *Sandra crosses to him. She loosens her red velvet cape and drops it to the floor at her feet. The white evening gown clings nakedly to her body.*

VAL. Don't stand there in front of me like that!

SANDRA. Why not? I'm just looking at you. You know what I feel when I look at you, Val? Always the weight of your body bearing me down.

VAL. *Christ.*

SANDRA. You think I ought to be ashamed to say that? Well, I'm not. I think that passion is something to be proud of. Val…

> *She touches his shoulder. He shoves her roughly away. The door opens and Myra enters.*

MYRA. Oh!

SANDRA. *(Casually.)* Hello, there. I thought you'd gone for the doctor.

MYRA. I couldn't get over the river. The bridge is out. What are *you* doing here?

SANDRA. I came here to give you a warning.

MYRA. A warning? Warning of what?

SANDRA. They've passed a law against passion. Our license has been revoked. We have to give it up or else be ostracized. Whoever has too much passion, we're going to be burned like witches because we know too much.

MYRA. What are you talking about?

SANDRA. Damnation! You see my lips have been touched by prophetic fire.

MYRA. I think they're also been touched by too much liquor. The store is closed.

SANDRA. I want to talk to you, Myra.

MYRA. Come back in the morning.

SANDRA. What morning? There isn't going to be any.

MYRA. I think there is.

SANDRA. That's just a case of unwarranted optimism. I have it on the very best of authority that time is all used up. There's no more time. *(With drunken exultation.)* The atmosphere is pregnant with disaster! Can't you feel it?

> *She laughs and suddenly clasps the palms of her hands to her ears.*

Now, I can even *hear* it!

VAL. What?

SANDRA. A battle in heaven. A battle of *angels* above us! And *thunder*! And *storm*!

> *She laughs wildly.*

MYRA. Sandra, I've had too much. I can't stand anything more. You go home now before I do something I shouldn't.

SANDRA. I believe you *would*. You'd fight like a *tiger* for him.

MYRA. Be careful, Sandra.

SANDRA. Yes, I can tell by looking at you in that mad dress with your eyes spitting fire like the Devil's, you've learned what I've learned, that there's nothing on earth you can do. No, nothing! But catch at whatever comes near you with both your hands, until your fingers are broken!

> *Sandra flings herself upon Val and kisses him with abandon. Myra springs at her like a tiger and slaps her fiercely across the face.*

MYRA. Leave him be, damn you, or I'll…

> *Sandra whimpers and staggers to the counter. Her head lolls forward and the dark hair slides over her face; she slips to her knees on the floor.*

Take her upstairs to my room. When dogs go mad, they ought to be locked and chained.

> *Val picks Sandra up and carries her up the stairs. The storm increases in violence; rain beats loud on the tin portico outside. There is a terribly loud thunder clap. Myra gasps. The electric current is disrupted and the lights dim out. Someone bangs at the door. Myra calls—*

The store's closed up!

MAN. It's me, Mrs. Torrance. Jim Talbott!

MYRA. Oh, Sheriff Talbott.

> *She opens the door.*

Is something the matter?

TALBOTT. Yes.

> *He enters, followed by a woman. There is something remarkably sinister about the woman's appearance. She is a hard, dyed blond in a dark suit. Her body is short and heavy but her face appears to have been burned thin by some consuming fever accentuated by the masklike makeup she wears and the falsely glittering gems on her fingers, which are knotted tight around her purse.*

This is Mrs. Regan from Waco, Texas.

WOMAN. Never mind about that. Where is the man that clerks here?

MYRA. Val?

WOMAN. Is that what he calls himself? In Waco he was known as Jonathan West.

MYRA. *(To the sheriff.)* What does this woman want here?

WOMAN. I want that man.

TALBOTT. That clerk of yours is wanted for rape in Texas.

MYRA. I'm sure you're mistaken.

WOMAN. Oh, no, I don't think I am. I've sent out descriptions of him to every town in the country. Canada, Mexico, even. The minute I got news of this shoe clerk I hopped a plane out of Waco. I feel pretty sure that I've finally tracked him down. Where is he? Where does he keep himself?

MYRA. He drove into Memphis.

WOMAN.   Two days before Easter? He suddenly drove into Memphis and left you without any help? That certainly does sound peculiar.

MYRA. I gave him his notice. He's gone.

WOMAN. I don't believe you.

MYRA. *(To the sheriff.)* This woman has got a pistol in her purse.

WOMAN. What if I have? You don't go hunting a dangerous animal down without any weapons.

> *She suddenly starts forward. She crosses to Vee's portrait.*

Come along, Sheriff, we're wasting time with this woman. She's telling us lies to protect him. The place to look is them sporting houses on Front Street.

> *She rushes from the store.*

TALBOTT. You're playing with fire, Mrs. Torrance.

> *He follows her out. Myra gasps and crosses to the door, bolting it shut. Val steps noiselessly out upon the upstairs landing and stares down at Myra. He descends a few steps with caution.*

VAL. *(On the stairs.)* Who was it?

MYRA. Sheriff Talbott.

VAL. *(Descending two steps.)* Who was the woman?

> *Myra stares up at him dumbly.*

Who was the woman with him?

MYRA. Val, don't act so excited.

VAL. Oh, it was her then.

MYRA. Yes. The woman from Waco.

VAL. Christ! I heard her voice but I thought I must be dreaming.

> *He suddenly catches his breath and darts down the stairs and toward the front door.*

MYRA. Where do you think you're goin'?

VAL. *Out!*

MYRA. Don't be a fool. You can't leave now.

VAL. Lock up that door!

MYRA. It's locked.

VAL. What happened to the lights?

MYRA. Went out in the storm. I'll turn on a lamp…

VAL. No. *Don't!*

MYRA. In the confectionery. They can't see in.

VAL. What did you tell her?

MYRA. That you'd gone into Memphis.

VAL. Did she believe you?

MYRA. No.

VAL. Oh, God, Myra, I've washed myself in mountain spring water to get the touch of her off my body. It's no good.

> *She picks up a lamp.*

MYRA. You're safe in here. They looked here once; they won't come back until morning.

VAL. *Safe?* She mentioned it in her description.

MYRA. Mentioned what?

VAL. Scars from burns on his legs. Afraid of fire. She'll have them *burn* me, Myra.

MYRA. Oh, Val, darling, don't act like a scared little boy.

VAL. I'm not so scared. I'm sick.

MYRA. I know how you feel.

VAL. Like something was crawling on me. Something that crawled up out of the basement of my brain. And now she has—She's *here*!

MYRA. *(Pityingly.)* Oh, Val, stay there. I'm going to fix you a drink. The rain has made the air colder. Don't you feel it?

VAL. No.

MYRA. I do. I seem to be shaking a little. I guess my blood's too thin. I'm leaving here with you tonight!

VAL. No.

MYRA. Oh, yes, I *am*. I've *got* to. As soon as the storm slacks up.

VAL. *(Rising.)* Myra…

MYRA. Give me a nickel; I want to play the Victrola.

VAL. Myra, you're…

MYRA. No. Never mind. Oh, the electricity's out. Wait just a minute.

VAL. Myra, you've got to…

MYRA. *Shhh!*

> *She comes back in.*

When I was a girl, I was always expecting something tremendous to happen. Maybe not this time but next time. I used to dance all night, come home drunk at daybreak and tiptoe barefooted up the back stairs. The sky used to be so white in the early mornings. You know it's been a long time since I've even noticed what color the sky is at daybreak. Traveling on a lonely road all night in an open car I guess you'd notice such things. I'd enjoy that. I could point them out to you while you were driving the car. I'd say, "Look, Val, here's something to put in the book!" "What is it?" I'd say, "It's white!" "What is?" "The sky is!" "Oh," you'd say, "is it?" "Yes," I'd say, "it is, it is, it *is!*" And you would have to believe me!

> *She clings to him; Val breaks away from her.*

VAL. I got to go by myself. I couldn't take anyone with me.

MYRA. Would I make the desert crowded?

VAL. Yes, you would. You'd make it crowded, Myra.

MYRA. Oh, my God, I thought the desert was *big*.

> *She goes to the confectionery and comes back out with a bottle.*

How much do you want? Three fingers? What was I…? Oh yes, yes, I wanted to tell you. We used to have a little fig tree between the house and the orchard. It never bore any fruit, they said it was barren. Time went by, spring after useless spring and it almost started to die. Then one day, I discovered a small green fig on the tree they said wouldn't bear. I ran through the orchard, I ran through the fields, shouting, "Oh Father, it's going to bear, the fig tree is going to bear. It seemed such a wonderful thing after those ten barren springs for the little fig tree to bear. It called for a celebration. I ran to a closet, I opened a box that we kept Christmas ornaments in, I took them out; glass bells, glass birds, tinsel, icicles, stars and I hung the little fig tree with them. I decorated the fig tree with glass bells and glass birds, with silver icicles and stars because it won the battle and would bear. Unpack the box. Unpack the box with the Christmas ornaments in it and put them on me: glass bells, and glass birds and stars and tinsel and snow.

VAL. *(Sharply.)* What do you mean?

MYRA. I mean that I'm not barren. Not anymore!

VAL. You're making this up!

MYRA. No, Val! You see, being clever, Val, isn't enough when you're up against something as big as life is. Sure, you can make keys for a door. That's clever, Val, but somebody comes along and breaks the door down. That's life! And that's what happened to me. Oh, God, I knew that I wouldn't be barren when we went together that first time. I felt it already, stirring up inside me, beginning to live! Here. Here's your drink.

> *He stares at her dumbly.*

Take it!

> *She thrusts it into his hand. Jabe knocks.*

VAL. Jabe's knocking.

MYRA. Don't you think that I hear him? Knock, knock, knock! It sounds like bones, like death, and that's what it is. Ahh, my flesh always crawled when he touched me. Yes, but I stood it, though. I guess I knew in my heart that it wouldn't go on forever. When you come in off the road and asked for a job, I said to myself, "This is it, this is what you been waiting for, Myra!" So I said with my eyes, "Stay here, stay here, for the love of God, stay here." And you did, you stayed. He started dying upstairs, when I started coming to life. It was like a battle had gone on between us those ten years, and I, the living, had beaten him, the dead one, back to the grave he climbed out of! Since then all decency's left me, I've stood like a woman naked with nothing but love—love, love.

> *She clings to him fiercely.*

VAL. Let go of me, Myra.

> *He shoves her roughly away.*

You're like the woman from Waco. The way you…

MYRA. *(Slowly she crosses to the door.)* If you try to leave here without me, I'll call for the sheriff!

VAL. That's what she did.

MYRA. *I'll* do it, *too*. Strike me in the face so I can scream. "I've won, I've won, Mr. Death. I'm going to bear."

> *She catches at him again, he breaks loose, she utters a choked cry. The door slams open on the landing. At this instant a flickering match light appears on the stairs and spills down them and across the floor. Heavy dragging footsteps and hoarse breathing are heard. Myra, whispering:*

Christ in Heaven, what's that?

> *The ghastly, phantomlike effect of this entrance is dramatically underlined. Jabe's shadow precedes him down the stairs and his approach has the slow, clumping fatality of the traditional spook's. He is a living symbol of death, as Myra has described him. He wears a purple bathrobe which hangs shroudlike about his figure and his face is a virtual death mask. Just as he appears in full view in the stairwell, the match which he holds under his face flickers out and disappears from view, swallowed in darkness like a vanished apparition. Myra, horrified, incredulous:*

Jabe.

JABE. *(Hoarsely.)* Yes, it's me!

> *He strikes another match and this time his face wears a grotesque, grinning expression.*

I didn't have much luck at knocking on the floor.

MYRA. *(Dazed.)* I didn't hear you.

JABE. Naw?

MYRA. The storm made too much noise.

JABE. Aw, absorbed in the storm.

MYRA. Yes.

JABE. Lamp light, huh?

MYRA. Yes, the lights went out when that awful lightning struck.

JABE. Your dress is torn open.

MYRA. You did that, Jabe, when I tried to give you morphine.

JABE. I thought you might give me too much.

MYRA. How did you get out of bed?

JABE. The usual way. Why? Does that seem remarkable to you?

MYRA. Yes. I didn't know you was able to.

JABE. You always been too optimistic about my condition.

> *Myra gasps involuntarily with loathing. Jabe laughs hoarsely.*

I'm okay now. I'm not going to cash my chips in yet for a while.

> *Val coughs uneasily and clears his throat.*

MYRA. Jabe—Jabe, this is Val Xavier.

JABE. You don't need to introduce me. I know him; I'm payin' his wages. *(To Val.)* Myra here seems to think I had a tumor on the brain and they cut the brain out an' left the tumor.

> *He laughs again and Myra repeats her involuntary gasp of loathing.*

Gimme that lamp; I wanta look at the stock.

MYRA. Here. We finished straightening up. Val couldn't go home in the storm so we took advantage of the extra time.

JABE. Uh-huh.

> *He takes the candle and goes unsteadily toward the confectionery. He passes through the archway; the pale walls hung with artificial blossoms have an eery effect in candlelight. The confectionery has a misty, flickering unreal pallor like a region of death, and Jabe in his long dark robe stands at the entrance like the very Prince of Darkness. He hesitates as though he senses that deathlike quality himself.*

Hell. It looks like a goddam honky-tonk since you done it over!

> *He moves resolutely on into the room.*

MYRA. *(Under her breath.)* Oh, God, I can't stand it, Val. I'm going to scream! Say something to him. Don't stand there doing nothing!

VAL. What should I say to him?

MYRA. Oh, I don't know—anything!

JABE. How about a little pinball game? Would you like to play one, Mr. Whatsit?

MYRA. Answer him!

VAL. *(Inaudibly.)* No.

JABE. Huh? Can't you talk out loud in there?

VAL. *(Shouting.)* No! No!

MYRA. Shhh!

JABE. I think I'll shoot a few.

VAL. Give me my wages. Let me get out.

   Val moves towards the counter, but Myra blocks him.

MYRA. You can't leave me alone with him, would you?

JABE. Hot damn. I clicked on three.

MYRA. You couldn't be such a coward.

VAL. Let go of my arm.

JABE. Twenty-five hundred, Myra.

VAL. This place is shrinking; the walls are closing in!

JABE. Thirty-five. Forty-five.

MYRA. Give me time, darling. A little more time.

   Val tears loose.

JABE. Fifty!

MYRA. I swear to God, I won't let you.

JABE. Right down the middle aisle, twice straight.

VAL. Let go!

JABE. Sixty-five, seventy.

MYRA. You've got to stick with me, Val.

VAL. Don't have to do nothing. I'm going!

JABE. Buzzards! Buzzards!!!! I hear you croaking in there. You think you've got a corpse to feed on, but you ain't! I'm going to live, Myra.

   Myra's hysteria is released. She laughs wildly and rushes to
   the doorway.

MYRA. Oh, no, you're not; no, you're not! You're going to die, Jabe. You're rotten with death already!

JABE. *(Shouting.)* Die, am I?

MYRA. Yes, and I'm glad, I'm *glad*, I'm planning a celebration! I'm going to wear Christmas ornaments in my hair! Because I'm not barren. I've gotten death out of me and now I've taken life in! Yes, oh, yes, I've got *life* in me—in here!

> *She clasps her hands over her stomach.*

I'm way, way, way up *high*! And you can't drag me *down*! Not anymore, *Mr. Death*! We're through with each other.

> *She laughs in wild exultance, then suddenly covers her face and runs sobbing back to Val. She is terrified.*

Val!

> *She clutches his arm. He breaks away and crosses toward the front door of the store.*

VAL. It's finished!

> *He goes to the cash register, rings it open. Jabe creeps in with the lantern, unseen by them, and steals towards the hardware counter.*

MYRA. (*Screaming at him wildly, completely distracted.*) What are you doing? You're robbing the store!

VAL. I'm taking my wages out.

MYRA. You're robbing the store; I won't let you!

> *She rushes to the phone and shouts into it. Jabe is loading a revolver.*

Give me the sheriff's house. The store's being robbed! The clerk is robbing the store. He's running off with the money; you got to stop him!

> *Jabe's face is livid with hatred and he holds the revolver, which he levels carefully at Myra, holding the candle above him to give a light.*

JABE. Buzzards!

> *He fires. The first shot strikes Myra. She utters a smothered cry and clutches at the wall. Val springs at him and wrests the revolver from his grasp.*

VAL. You shot her.

JABE. (*Slowly, panting.*) Naw. *You* shot her. Didn'tja hear her shouting your name on the phone? She said you was robbing the store! They'll come here an' burn you for it! Buzzards!

He turns slowly and staggers out the front door. His voice is heard shouting wildly against the wind. Val gasps, slams the door, and bolts it, the revolver still in his grasp. Myra moves out from the shadow of the wall with a slight, sobbing breath.

The clerk shot my wife!

VAL. Myra!

MYRA. Yes.

VAL. How bad?

MYRA. I don't know. I don't feel nothing at all. There's nothing but death in me now.

VAL. I'll call for the doctor!

MYRA. There's no way to get any doctor. Go on, look out for yourself, get away! I don't need anyone now…

She staggers out from the wall.

Some things are enemies of light and there is a battle between them in which some fall!

The confectionery suddenly blooms into soft springlike radiance as the electric current resumes.

Oh, look! The lights have come on in the confectionery!

She staggers through the archway.

That's what I wanted! Not death, but David—the orchard across from Moon Lake!

She advances a few more steps and disappears from sight. Her body is heard falling. Val crosses to the archway.

VAL. Myra! Myra!

The lights flicker and go out. Now the clamor of the crowd is heard distantly. Outside we see flashlights roaming and hear mumbles. Val runs to the basement. Enter Pee Wee, First, Second, and Third Man. Pee Wee moves to the basement.

PEE WEE. Downstairs, he's down there in the back room.

FIRST MAN. Rope, get rope.

SECOND MAN. Get rope from the hardware section.

THIRD MAN. I've got something better than rope.

FIRST MAN. A *blowtorch.*

PEE WEE. Come on. What the hell are we waiting for!

> *They all move downstairs. Cassandra enters singing "Kyrie Eleison." Val screams from below. The Conjure Man enters from the basement.*

SANDRA. What have you got there, Uncle? Come here and let me see. Oh yes, his snakeskin jacket. I'll give you a gold ring for it. Wild things leave skin behind them. They leave clean skins and teeth and white bones behind them and these are tokens passed from one to another so that the fugitive kind can always follow their kind.

> *The woman from Waco and Sheriff appear at the door.*

WOMAN. She's got his jacket, stop her.

TALBOTT. Don't move. Don't move.

> *Sandra walks out.*

WOMAN. Stop, stop, stop.

> *The woman from Waco shoots. Sandra laughs and the lights go out.*

CURTAIN

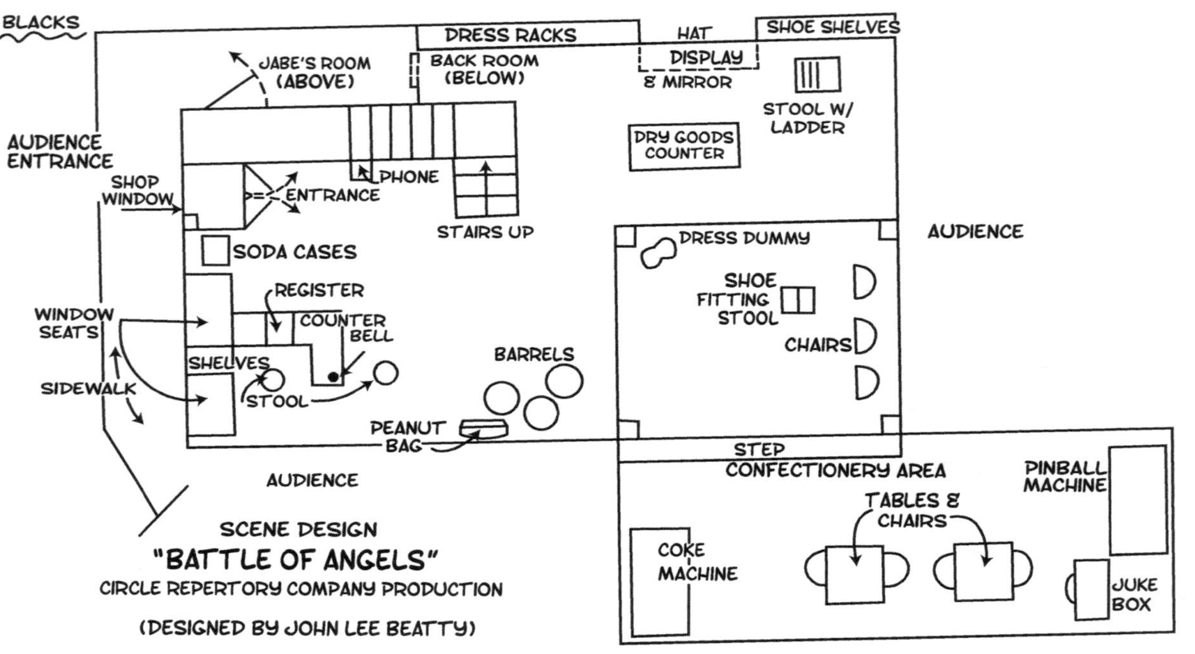

BLACKS
DRESS RACKS
HAT
SHOE SHELVES
JABE'S ROOM (ABOVE)
BACK ROOM (BELOW)
DISPLAY & MIRROR
STOOL W/ LADDER
AUDIENCE ENTRANCE
DRY GOODS COUNTER
SHOP WINDOW
PHONE
ENTRANCE
STAIRS UP
SODA CASES
DRESS DUMMY
AUDIENCE
REGISTER
COUNTER BELL
SHOE FITTING STOOL
CHAIRS
WINDOW SEATS
SHELVES
STOOL
BARRELS
SIDEWALK
PEANUT BAG
STEP
CONFECTIONERY AREA
PINBALL MACHINE
AUDIENCE
SCENE DESIGN
"BATTLE OF ANGELS"
CIRCLE REPERTORY COMPANY PRODUCTION
(DESIGNED BY JOHN LEE BEATTY)
TABLES & CHAIRS
COKE MACHINE
JUKE BOX

PROPERTY LIST

(Use this space to make props lists for your production)

SOUND EFFECTS
(Use this space to create sound effects lists for your production)

script in any way—including casting against the writer's intentions for characters, removing or changing "bad" words, or making other cuts however small—without permission, they are breaking the law. And, perhaps more importantly, changing an artist's work. Please don't do that!

We are thrilled that this play has made it into your hands. We hope you love it as much as we do, and thank you for helping us keep the American theater alive and vital.

Note on Songs/Recordings, Images, or Other Production Design Elements

Be advised that Dramatists Play Service, Inc., neither holds the rights to nor grants permission to use any songs, recordings, images, or other design elements mentioned in the play. It is the responsibility of the producing theater/organization to obtain permission of the copyright owner(s) for any such use. Additional royalty fees may apply for the right to use copyrighted materials.

For any songs/recordings, images, or other design elements mentioned in the play, works in the public domain may be substituted. It is the producing theater/organization's responsibility to ensure the substituted work is indeed in the public domain. Dramatists Play Service, Inc., cannot advise as to whether or not a song/arrangement/recording, image, or other design element is in the public domain.

NOTE ON BILLING

Anyone receiving permission to produce BATTLE OF ANGELS is required to give credit to the Author as sole and exclusive Author of the Play on the title page of all programs distributed in connection with performances of the Play and in all instances in which the title of the Play appears for purposes of advertising, publicizing or otherwise exploiting the Play and/or a production thereof. The name of the Author must appear on a separate line, in which no other name appears, immediately beneath the title and in size of type equal to 50% of the size of the largest, most prominent letter used for the title of the Play. No person, firm or entity may receive credit larger or more prominent than that accorded the Author. The following acknowledgment must appear on the title page in all programs distributed in connection with performances of the Play:

BATTLE OF ANGELS is presented by arrangement with
Dramatists Play Service, Inc. on behalf of
The University of the South, Sewanee, Tennessee.

ALL TENNESSEE WILLIAMS PLAYS

The Play must be performed as published in the DPS authorized edition. It is understood that there will be no nudity in the Play unless specifically indicated in the script and that nothing in the stage presentation or stage business will alter the spirit of the Play as written.